AFTER A WAR

Longman

AFTER A WAR
R. A. Marshall

Longman Paul Limited
182–190 Wairau Road, Auckland 10, New Zealand

Longman Cheshire Pty Limited
346 St Kilda Road Melbourne Australia 3004

Associated companies, branches, and representatives
throughout the world

Copyright © 1975 Longman Paul/Longman Australia

First published in 1975
Reprinted 1979

ISBN 0 582 68239 8

Filmset in Hong Kong by Asco Trade Typesetting Limited
Printed in Hong Kong by Wah Cheong Printing Press Ltd.

Contents

Acknowledgements

PART I
The Great War, 1914–1918

ROGER McGOUGH
  On Picnics   5
HENRY NEWBOLT
  Vitai Lampada   6
THOMAS HARDY
  Drummer Hodge   6
LAURENCE BINYON
  From The Fourth of August   6
THOMAS HARDY
  From Men Who March Away   7
EDWARD SHANKS
  The Old Soldiers   7
GILBERT FRANKAU
  The Deserter   7

RUPERT BROOKE
  The Dead   7
  Peace   8
  The Soldier   8
W.N. HODGSON
  England to Her Sons   8
RUDYARD KIPLING
  Common Form   8
ROBERT GRAVES
  Two Fusiliers   9
RUDYARD KIPLING
  A Dead Statesman   9
JOHN McRAE
  In Flanders Fields   9
ALAN SEEGER
  Rendezvous   11
WILLOUGHBY WEAVING
  Flanders   11
RICHARD ADLINGTON
  Bombardment   11
ROBERT PALMER
  How Long, O Lord?   12
ISAAC ROSENBERG
  The Dying Soldier   12
EDGELL RICKWORD
  Trench Poets   12
IVOR GURNEY
  The Target   13
RUDYARD KIPLING
  Unknown Female Corpse   13
RICHARD ALDINGTON
  Soliloquy I   13
  Soliloquy II   13
FREDERIC MANNING
  A Shell   14
  The Face   14
ROBERT GRAVES
  The Leveller   14

SIEGFRIED SASSOON
    Died of Wounds 15
    Base Details 15
A.P. HERBERT
    After the Battle 15
WILFRID GIBSON
    Breakfast 16
SIEGFRIED SASSOON
    Blighters 16
    The Dug-Out 16
    Lamentations 16
EDWARD THOMAS
    A Private 16
RUDYARD KIPLING
    The Favour 16
A.A. MILNE
    From Gold Braid 18
WILFRED OWEN
    The Next War 18
    The Parable of the Old Man and the Young 18
WILFRED OWEN
    Futility 18
SIEGFRIED SASSOON
    Does it Matter? 19
CARL SANDBURG
    A.E.F. 19
SIEGFRIED SASSOON
    Dreamers 19
    The General 19
W.N. EWER
    Five Souls 20
WILFRID GIBSON
    The Bayonet 20
RUDYARD KIPLING
    Bombed in London 21
    A Son 21

HERBERT READ
    Ypres 21
GILBERT FRANKAU
    Poison 21
WILFRED OWEN
    Anthem for Doomed Youth 22
    At a Calvary near the Ancre 22
    The Send-Off 22
    Strange Meeting 23
SIEGFRIED SASSOON
    Attack 23
LAURENCE BINYON
    For the Fallen 24
WILFRED OWEN
    Dulce et Decorum Est 24
SIEGFRIED SASSOON
    Aftermath 25
OSBERT SITWELL
    This Generation 25
    From How Shall we Rise to Greet the Dawn 25
HERBERT ASQUITH
    Nightfall 25
PHILIP JOHNSTONE
    High Wood 27
SIEGFRIED SASSOON
    Twelve Months After 27
W.B. YEATS
    Death 27

PART II
The Lost Peace, 1919–1939

JOHN DONNE
    Meditation 17 30
W.H. AUDEN
    From Journey to a War 1939 31

ROY CAMPBELL
    Christ in Uniform   31
C. DAY LEWIS
    From Overtures to Death 1938—Newsreel   31
JOHN CORNFORD
    Full Moon at Tierz: Before the Storming of Huesca   32
DYLAN THOMAS
    Do Not Go Gentle into that Good Night   32
    And Death Shall Have No Dominion   33
    The Hand that Signed the Paper   33
SIEGFRIED SASSOON
    On Passing the New Menin Gate   35
LAURIE LEE
    Words Asleep   35
JOHN CORNFORD
    A Letter from Aragon   35
STEPHEN SPENDER
    Fall of a City   36
HERBERT READ
    Bombing Casualties in Spain   36
W.H. AUDEN
    Refugee Blues   37

PART III
Poetry of the Second World War 1939—1945
HERBERT PALMER
    From Air Raid   40
RANDELL JARRELL
    Death of the Ball Turret Gunner   41
JOHN MANIFOLD
    The Recruit   43
IAN SERAILLIER
    The New Learning   43
PAUL SCOTT
    Tell Us the Tricks   44

JOHN PUDNEY
    For Johnny   44
    Missing
JOHN BAYLISS
    Reported Missing   45
JOHN PUDNEY
    Air Gunner   45
    Combat Report   45
NIGEL WEIR
    War   45
DAVID BOURNE
    Operations Calling   46
NORMAN HAMPSON
    Corvette   46
JOHN WEDGE
    Action Stations   46
ALAN ROSS
    Destroyers in the Arctic   47
ALAN ROSS
    Naval Base   48
RANDALL JARRELL
    A War   48
CHARLES CAUSLEY
    Song of the Dying Gunner   48
DONALD BAIN
    Poem   48
EDITH SITWELL
    Still Falls the Rain   49
R.N. CURREY
    Unseen Fire   51
DENTON WELCH
    Rural Raid   51
DYLAN THOMAS
    A Refusal to Mourn the Death, by Fire, of a Child in London   51
ALUN LEWIS
    All Day It Has Rained   52

SIDNEY KEYES
  War Poet   52
RAYNER HEPPENSTALL
  Instead of a Carol   52
KEITH DOUGLAS
  Simplify Me When I'm Dead   53
RICHARD EBERHART
  The Fury of Aerial Bombardment   53
STEPHEN SPENDER
  Memento   53
ANONYMOUS
  Homesick   55
PATRICK SAVAGE
  Second Autumn   55

PART IV
The Age of Anxiety 1945 —
VERNON SCANNELL
  From Remembrance Day   57
ROGER McGOUGH
  A Square Dance   57
DOMINIC BEHAN
  From The Patriot Game   59
ROGER McGOUGH
  Why Patriots are a Bit Nuts in the Head   60
ALAN COVEN
  The Soldier   60
BUFFY ST MARIE
  Universal Soldier   61
KARL SHAPIRO
  From Recapitulations 13   63
JAMES K. BAXTER
  Returned Soldier   63
KARL SHAPIRO
  From Recapitulations 2   64

E.E. Cummings
  Thanksgiving (1956)   64
RANDALL JARRELL
  Jews at Haifa   65
D.J. ENRIGHT
  The Monuments of Hiroshima   67
SPIKE HAWKINS
  Salad Days 1914   67
M.K. JOSEPH
  Victory March   67
MICHAEL IVENS
  Haifa Bay in the Morning   68
R.A.K. MASON
  Sonnet to MacArthur's Eyes   69
JOHN PUDNEY
  Twentieth-Century Mother   69
JAMES K. BAXTER
  From Elegy for an Unknown Soldier   70
  Pig Island Letters (8)   70
e.e. cummings
  o to be in finland   70
ERNESTO CHE GUEVARA
  Song to Fidel   71
FERNANDO GORDILLO CERVANTES
  A Dead Youth   72
  The Price of a Country   72
JAVIER HERAUD
  Poem   72
MARCO ANTONIO FLORES
  Havana 1959   72
ROGER McGOUGH
  Snipers   73
  On Picnics   73
  Mother the Wardrobe is Full of Infantrymen   74
LINDA NEWTON
  Lance-Corporal Dixon   74

ROBERT GRAVES
The Enlisted Man 74
YEVGENY YEVTUSHENKO
Weddings 75
Later 75
ADRIAN HENRI
Great War Poems 76
BRIAN PATTEN
Sleep Now 76
MICHAEL HAMBURGER
After a War 77
ADRIAN MITCHELL
Fifteen Million Plastic Bags 77
Order Me a Transparent Coffin 78
BERNARD KOPS
Peach, Plum, or Apricot 78
JOHN LEHMANN
This Excellent Machine 78
YEVGENY YEVTUSHENKO
Telling Lies to the Young is Wrong 80
PETER APPLETON
The Responsibility 80
WILLIAM SOUTAR
Parable 81
BRIAN PATTEN
Little Johnny's Confession 81
Little Johnny's Foolish Invention 82
DENISE LEVERTOV
What Were They Like? 83

EDWIN BROCK
Five Ways to Kill a Man 83
ADRIAN MITCHELL
To Whom it May Concern 85
ROGER JONES
Imperial War Museum 85
GEORGE MacBETH
Missile Commander 86
ADRIAN MITCHELL
Norman Morrison 86
ALISTAIR PATERSON
Soldiers 87
HONE TUWHARE
No Ordinary Sun 88
GEORGE STARBUCK
Of Late 88
PETER PORTER
Your Attention Please 89
ERNO MULLER
Assault 90
W.S. MERWIN
When the War is Over 90
PETER PORTER
Somme and Flanders 90

Resource Material 91
Index of first lines 94
Index of Poets 97

Acknowledgements

We are grateful to the following for permission to reproduce copyright material:
George Allen & Unwin Ltd for 'Little Johnny's Foolish Invention', 'Little Johnny's Confession', and 'Sleep Now' by Brian Patten from *Little Johnny's Confession*; and 'All Day It Has Rained' by Alun Lewis from *Raider's Dawn*; Basil Blackwell for 'Flanders' by Willoughby Weaving from *The Star Fields and Other Poems*; Dominic Behan for an extract from 'The Patriot Game'; The Bodley Head for 'Christ in Uniform' from *The Collected Poems of Roy Campbell*, Volume 1, and for 'Operations Calling' from *Poems* by David Bourne; John Bayliss for his poem 'Reported Missing'; Curtis Brown Ltd for 'Gold Braid' by A.A. Milne from *The Sunny Side*; Jonathon Cape Ltd and New Directions Publishing Corporation for 'What Were They Like' from *The Sorrow Dance* by Denise Levertov; Jonathon Cape Ltd, the Executors, and Pat Sloan for 'Full Moon at Tierz: Before the Storming of Huesca' and 'A Letter From Aragon' from *John Cornford: A Memoir*; Jonathon Cape Ltd for 'Order me a Transparent Coffin and Dig My Crazy Grave' and 'Fifteen Million Plastic Bags' from *Poems* by Adrian Mitchell, and for an extract from *Catch—22* by Joseph Heller; Cape Golliard Press, and Edward Dorn and Gordon Brotherston, translators, for 'A Dead Youth' and 'The Price of a Country' by Fernando Gordillo Cervantes, 'Havana 1959' by Marco Antonio Flores, 'Poem' by Javier Heraud, and 'Song to Fidel' by Ernesto Che Guevara all from *Our Word*; Cape Golliard Press for 'Norman Morrison' and 'To Whom It May Concern' from *Out Loud* by Adrian Mitchell; Chatto & Windus Ltd and author for 'The Monuments of Hiroshima' by D.J. Enright, and 'The Fury of Aerial Bombardment' from *Collected Poems 1930–1960* by Richard Eberhart; Chatto & Windus Ltd and the Author's Literary Estate for 'The Dying Soldier' from *Poems* by Isaac Rosenburg; Chatto and Windus Ltd and the Executors of the Estate of Harold Owen for 'Strange Meeting', 'The Parable of The Old Man and The Young', 'Anthem for Doomed Youth', 'The Send-Off', 'Dulce et Docorum Est', 'Futility', 'The Next War', and 'At Calvary Near Ancre' from *The Collected Poems of Wilfred Owen*, ed. C. Day Lewis; The Clarendon Press, Oxford, for 'Lance-Corporal Dixon' by Linda Newton and 'Assault' by Erno Muller both from *Every Man Will Shout*, © 1964 Oxford University Press; Rosica Colin Ltd for 'Soliloquy 1', 'Soliloquy 2', and 'Bombardment' by Richard Aldington from *Collected Poems*; Collins Publishers for an extract from *A Precocious Autobiography* by Yevgeny Yevtushenko; Constable Publishers for 'Rendezvous' by Alan Seegar from *Poems*; J.M. Dent & Sons Ltd and the Trustees for 'A Refusal to Mourn', 'The Hand that Signed the Paper', 'And Death Shall Have No Dominion', and 'Do Not Go Gentle into that Good Night' by Dylan Thomas from *Collected Poems*; Dent and Putnam for 'Twentieth Century Mother', 'Air Gunner', 'For Johnny', 'Missing', and 'Combat Report' by John Pudney from *Spill Out* and *Collected Poems*; Denis Dobson for 'The Recruit' by John Manifold from Selected Verse; Gerald Duckworth & Co. for 'This Generation' by Osbert Sitwell from *Collected Poems and Satires* and 'How Shall We Rise' from *Selected Poems Old and New*; W.N. Ewer for 'Five Souls'; Enitharmon Press, London, and poet for 'Trench Poets' by Edgell Rickword from *Collected Poems* (1947); Faber & Faber for 'Jews at Haifa', 'A War' and 'Death of the Ball Turret Gunner' by Randall Jarrell from *The Complete Poems*, 'Ypres' and 'Bombing Casualties in Spain' by Herbert Read from *Collected Poems*, 'Sonnets from China' XII ('Here war is harmless like a monument'), and 'Refugee Blues' by W.H. Auden from *Collected Shorter Poems 1927–1957*, 'Fall of a City' and 'Memento' by Stephen Spender from *Collected Poems 1928–1953*, 'Simplify Me When I'm Dead' by Keith Douglas from *Collected Poems*, extract from *Memoirs of an Infantry Officer* by Siegfried Sassoon, and 'War' by A.N.C. Weir from *Verses of a Fighter Pilot*; Faber & Faber and Mrs Myfanwy Thomas for 'A Private' by Edward Thomas from *Collected Poems*; Favill for 'Tell Us the Tricks' by Paul Scott from the *Poets Now* series; Mrs Gilbert Frankau for 'The Deserter' from *The Judgement of Valhalla* and 'Poison' from *Poems of War and Peace* both by Gilbert Frankau; Robert Graves for 'The Enlisted Man' from *Collected Poems 1959*, and 'Two Fusiliers' and 'The Leveller' both from *Poems 1914–1927*; Michael Hamburger for his poem 'After A War' from *In Flashlight*, Northern House Pamphlet Poets; Rupert Hart-Davie for 'Song of the Dying Gunner' by Charles Causley from *Union Street*, Hand and Flower Press, and 'When the War is over' by W.S. Merwin from *The Lice*; Hamish Hamilton, London for extract from Hiroshima © by John Hersey 1947, 1966; Norman Hampson for his poem 'Corvette' from *More Poems from the Forces*; Harcourt Brace Jovanovich for 'A.E.F.' from *Smoke and Steel* by Carl Sandburg, copyright 1920 by Harcourt Brace Jovanovich Inc., copyright 1948 by Carl Sandburg, reprinted by permission of the publishers; Rayner Heppenstall for his poem 'Instead of a Carol' from *Poems*; Lady G. Herbert for 'After a Battle' by Sir Alan Herbert from *The Bomber Gypsy*, Methuen; Hodder and Stoughton for 'How Long O Lord?' by Robert Palmer from *The Life of Robert Palmer*,

Lady Laura Ridding; The Hogarth Press and poet for 'Words Asleep' from *The Sun My Monument* by Laurie Lee; Hope, Leresche & Steele and the poet for 'A Square Dance', 'Snipers', 'Why Patriots are a Bit Nuts in the Head', 'Mother the Wardrobe if Full of Infantrymen', and 'On Picnics' by Roger McGough from *Penguin Modern Poets 10*; Michael Ivens for his poem 'Haifa Bay in the Morning'; M.K. Joseph for his poem 'Victory March' from *Imaginary Islands*, 1950; John Lehmann for his poem 'This Excellent Machine' from *Collected Poems*, Eyre & Spottiswoode; Longman Paul and the poet for 'No Ordinary Sun' from *No Ordinary Sun* by Hone Tuwhare; George Macbeth for his poem 'Missile Commander' from *Missile Commander*; MacGibbon & Kee Ltd for 'Thanksgiving (1956)' and 'o to be in finland' from *Complete Poems* Volume 11 by e.e. cummings; Macmillan & Co., Mrs George Bambridge, and the Macmillan Co. of Canada for 'Epitaphs of War' from *The Years Between* by Rudyard Kipling, 'Common Form', 'A Dead Statesman', 'A Son', 'Bombed in London', 'The Favour', and 'Unknown Female Corpse'; Macmillan, London and Basingstoke, and Mr M. Gibson for 'Breakfast' and 'The Bayonet' by Wilfred Gibson from *Collected Poems*; Macmillan, London and Basingstoke, and the Trustees for 'Drummer Hodge' and 'Men Who March Away' by Thomas Hardy and for 'The Old Soldiers' by Edward Shanks from *Poems 1912–32*; Macmillan, London and Basingstoke, and Mr M.B. Yeats for 'Death' from *The Collected Poems of W.B. Yeats*; John Murray and the poet for 'The Face' and 'The Shell' by Frederick Manning from *Eidola*; Mr Peter Newbolt for 'Vitai Lampada' from *Poems New and Old* by Sir Henry Newbolt; New Statesman for 'High Wood' by Philip Johnstone; The Trustees of the National Library of Scotland for 'Parable' by William Soutar; Oxford University for 'Pig Island Letters (8)' from *Pig Island Letters*, © Oxford University Press 1966 and 'Returned Soldier' from *In Fires Of No Return*, © Oxford University Press 1958, 'Elegy for an Unknown Soldier' from *The Rock Woman*, all by James K. Baxter; Herbert Palmer for an extract from his poem 'Air Raid 1917–18'; Pan Books Ltd for an extract from *Life is a Four Letter Word* Vol. 1 by Nicholas Monsarrat; A.I.H. Paterson for his poem 'Soldiers' from *Pacific Number* of *Poet* (India), March 1972; Peter Porter for his poems 'Your Attention Please' and 'Somme and Flanders' from *Penguin Modern Poets*; Pegasus Press Ltd for 'Sonnet to MacArthur's Eyes' by R.A.K. Mason; Penguin Books Ltd, author, and translators for 'Weddings', 'Later', and 'Telling Lies to the Young is Wrong' by Yevgeny Yevtushenko from *Yevtushenko: Selected Poems*, translated by Robin Milner-Gulland and Peter Levi, S.J., copyright © Robin Milner-Gulland and Peter Levi, 1962; Penguin Books Ltd and poet for 'Five Ways to Kill a Man' by Edwin Brock from *Penguin Modern Poets 8*; Punch Publications and Alan Foley Pty Ltd for 'If I Should Drool' by Alan Coven from *Pick of Punch*, and 'In Flanders Field' by John McRae both © Punch Publications, London; Random House, Inc. for 'Recapitulations 2', copyright 1946 by Karl Shapiro, from *Selected Poems* by Karl Shapiro, and 'Recapitulations 13', copyright 1943 by Karl Shapiro, from *Trial of a Poet and Other Poems* by Karl Shapiro; Deborah Rogers Ltd, London for 'Great War Poems' by Adrian Henri from *Penguin Modern Poets 10*, copyright © 1967 by Adrian Henri; Alan Ross for his poems 'Destroyers in the Artic' and 'Naval Base' from *Something of the Sea*, Verschoyle; Routledge & Kegan Paul Ltd and the poet for 'Unseen Fire' By R.N. Currey from *This Other Planet*; G.T. Sassoon for 'Base Details', 'Lamentations', 'The General', 'Blighters', 'Died of Wounds', 'Attack', 'Twelve Months After', 'Dreamers', 'Does it Matter?', 'The Dugout', 'Aftermath', and 'On Passing the New Menin Gate' by Siegfried Sassoon; Vernon Scanell for an extract from 'Remembrance Day'; Ian Serraillier for his poem 'The New Learning' from *Poems of this War*, Oxford; Sidgwick & Jackson Ltd and author for 'Nightfall' by Herbert Asquith from *Poems 1912–33*; The Society of Authors and Mrs Nicolete Gray on behalf of the Laurence Binyon Estate for 'The Fourth of August' from *The Four Years* and 'For the Fallen' (September 1914) by Laurence Binyon; John F.N. Wedge for his poem 'Action Stations' from *More Poems from the Forces*; University of Texas for 'Rural Raid' by Denton Welch; Donald Bain for his poem 'Poem'; Routledge & Kegan Paul Ltd for 'War Poet' by Sidney Keyes; Charles Skilton Publishing Group for 'Second Autumn' by Patrick Savage; Jonathan Cape Ltd, the Hogarth Press, and the Executors of the Estate of C. Day-Lewis for 'Newsreel' by C. Day-Lewis from *Collected Poems 1954*.

We are grateful to the following for permission to reproduce photographs: *The Age*, Melbourne (56, 84), Australian Army Public Relations (79), Australian War Memorial (17, 47, 59), Herald and Weekly Times Limited (66), Imperial War Museum, London (cover, 10, 38, 54), Radio Times Hulton Picture Library, London (xii, 26, 28, 30, 34), Ullstein Bilderdienst (42), and War Histories Collection, Alexander Turnbull Library, Wellington, New Zealand (50).

Part I THE GREAT WAR
1914-1918

The 'Old School' Poets

Many of the poets of the Great War were ex-public school boys, although naturally there were many exceptions—such as Ivor Gurney and Isaac Rosenberg. Despite the fact that critics now deride public schools, it is impossible not to notice the self command and discipline these young men showed—almost as if they had been geared for it—which in a way they had.

Only in England, one imagines, could Sir Henry Newbolt have written a poem such as 'Vitai Lampada', while in 'He Fell Among Thieves' another Clifton College boy bravely faces death—this time in far off Afghanistan;

> He saw the School Close, sunny and green,
> The runner beside him, the stand by the parapet wall,
> The distant tape, and the crowd roaring between.

The old nineteenth century ideas of warfare had not disappeared in 1914, and even the Boer War was still seen largely as a game in which the Away team must always be better supplied.

Before one criticises these men for mistakenly thinking the new war would be rather fun, it must be remembered there had been no major war for over a century, and in 1914 there was no indication that it would develop into the greatest major war on record.

Robert Graves referred to this period as a 'queer time' and realised the difficulty for young officers who one week had been safe at school, and the next, leading their men into battle—'The trouble is, things happen much too quick'.

In the end, 20 per cent of all eligible men from these public schools died in the fighting.

1914

Despite the multitude of works devoted to the subject, the question of responsibility for the outbreak of war in 1914 is still not settled. Once it was blamed on German aggressiveness and imperialism, but now in historical retrospect, it appears that the two systems of alliances, which had arisen in Europe prior to 1914, made the war inevitable. French sociologist Raymond Aron wrote in 1954 'The two camps alarmed each other and each tried to soothe its own fears by piling up defensive armaments'. Into this rode Archduke Franz Ferdinand to inspect the Bosnian Army at Sarajevo and, incidentally, (though he did not know it) to be assassinated.

The Early Years

The effect of propaganda, both at the outbreak of war and later on, was staggering—the numbers at reception centres could not at first be catered for, and many had to wait their turn. In France, however, the opposing armies were soon deadlocked, and although people at home were confidently assured that 'the boys will be home for Christmas!', which particular Christmas was not specified. The boys did not come home for Christmas in 1914 and in 1915 it was obvious that they would not be home that year either. The front in France was a stalemate. Diversionary expeditions began, to Gallipoli and Salonika, in an attempt to force the back door to Germany by destroying her Turkish ally.

1915 also saw the death of the first of the 'great' war poets—Rupert Brooke—who died en route to the Balkans. Already his poetry had had a tremendous impact—D.H. Lawrence described him as 'a Greek god under a Japanese sunshade', Dean Inge quoted his poems in Westminster, while Winston Churchill called him a modern Apollo. (Julian Grenfell was also a writer of the same idealistic school as Brooke—in 1914 he could write in a letter—'I adore War. It is like a big picnic without the objectlessness of a picnic!'.)

The Home Front 1915–16

As has been stated, the British made great use of propaganda in the war, from the 'Your Country Needs You' appeal on the famous Kitchener poster to the outlandish accusation that the Hun actually ate babies in Belgium. An appeal to the pride of the married man and his feeling for his children, 'What Did You Do in the Great War Daddy?' became, with slight variation (cf. Adrian Henri's 'Great War Poems'), a most popular catch-phrase. There is little doubt however, that the skilful use of British propaganda in the United States contributed to a great extent in turning popular feeling against Germany in favour of the Allies—thus paving the way for American involvement in the war.

Nicholas Monsarrat in his autobiography gives an interesting account of what both propaganda and war meant to an intelligent six year old at home on the sideline;

> 'All over by Christmas' wasn't said any more; instead, there was the big push, and Verdun and the Somme and Ypres (which Mother pronounced so beautifully, like a genteel hiccup), and poison gas, and a war to end war, and the Russian Steam-roller—a gay and splendid vehicle which I longed to see, and perhaps one day even to drive.
>
> There were the Dardanelles, and the U-boats which had sunk the *Lusitania* and drowned all the poor babies.
>
> There was gallant little Belgium. There was King and Country. There were land-girls (a sniff from Mother). There were Zeppelins which dropped bombs and murdered innocent people in their beds. There was the Kaiser, the most wicked man in the whole world. ('And to think he's a cousin!' said Mother especially outraged.) There were the Huns, and Tommies, and shell-shock. There was a terrible gun called a Big Bertha. There was an entirely new reason for finishing up every scrap of rice-pudding—'Think of the starving Belgians'.
>
> There was a famous naval victory at Jutland which, I was repeatedly told, should make me very proud of my (naval) uniform. I didn't need Jutland for that.
>
> More important than anyone, it seemed, there was Lord Kitchener, the man with the huge curling moustache and the pointing finger, whose posters said, at every street corner: 'Your King and Country Want YOU!' It was a black day for the household when we heard that he had been killed—mysteriously sunk in the North Sea. 'I told you so!' said Mother—and it was true; she had told us so, often enough. 'Spies! How did they know he was on that ship? German spies!

The Turning Point

The turning point (although not then obvious) came in 1916—the year of the Battle of the Somme, and Jutland. The Liberals were defeated after a crisis in the munitions industry and a great rise in prices. The national hero, Lord Kitchener, was drowned in H.M.S. *Hampshire*—his death resulted in the appointment of the most controversial of war leaders, Field-Marshal Sir Douglas Haig. In 1916 also came the first conscription, for by now the original force was totally inadequate to keep pace with the slaughter.

With Haig in command it was not long before poets' voices were raised in protest. Although poets like Sir Henry Newbolt admired the man, people such as Robert Graves and Siegfried Sassoon repudiated his contempt for the lives of his men. The choice of Flanders for the attack in 1917 was especially culpable when the rain, the mud, and the cold, were nearly as bad as the enemy—while Haig excused himself stating that 'there was no reason to anticipate the heavy rainfall'.

Leon Wolff, in *In Flanders Fields,* lays blame on Haig in his account of the campaign, and his most recent biographer, John Terraine, completely fails to exonerate him. An ironic poem, which sums up the feeling toward Haig—incidentally the founder of Poppy Day—is Sassoon's 'The General' in which his indifference to the fate of his men is smartly hit off:

> But he did for them both with his plan of attack

Adrian Henri writing in the 1960s reminded us that Haig is still neither forgiven nor forgotten, for his actions of over fifty years ago. In 'Great War Poems' he reverses the popular advertising phrase;

> DON'T BE VAGUE—ASK FOR HAIG!

to an ironic;

> DON'T BE VAGUE—BLAME GENERAL HAIG!

Siegfried Sassoon

Generally, Sassoon is one of the most widely recognised and well known of the war poets. His early war poetry, like that of many poets, was embarrassing in its idealism, but Sassoon was one poet who completely changed, later becoming entirely disillusioned with the entire war. In the end he refused further active service, and to avoid court-martial, was sent to Craiglockhart in Scotland, a hospital which treated shell-shock cases.

Sassoon's poetry is forceful and direct, and in many cases is lacking completely in subtlety and control. He tells life as it was, he does not gloss over any of the unpleasantries of the Front, and in *Memoirs of an Infantry Officer* one can find the incidents which inspired some of his poems. 'Lamentations' for example stemmed from the following incident:

> I reported myself at the 5th Infantry Base Depot at Rouen...the Adjutant advised me to draw some blankets... when I opened a door and found myself in the Guard Room. A man, naked to the waist, was kneeling in the middle of the floor, clutching at his chest and weeping uncontrollably. The Guards were standing around with embarrassed looks, and the Sergeant was beside him, patient and unpitying. While he was leading me to the blanket store I asked him what was wrong. 'Why, Sir, the man's been under detention for assaulting the military police, and now 'e's just 'ad news of his brother being killed. Seems to take it to 'eart more than most would. 'Arf crazy 'e's been, tearing 'is clothes off and cursing the War and the Fritzes. Almost like a shell-shock case, 'e seems. It's his third time out. A Blighty one doesn't last a man long nowadays, Sir.' As I went off into the gloom I could still hear the uncouth howlings.

Another poem 'Died of Wounds' was prompted by an unforgettable experience while in hospital;

> The wind came from the direction of the Somme, and I could hear the remote thudding of the guns. Everyone in the ward seemed to be asleep except the boy whose bed had screens round it...Ever since he was brought in he'd been continually calling to the nurse on duty. Throughout the day this had gradually got on everyone's nerves, for the ward was already full of uncontrollable gasps and groans. Once I had caught a glimpse of his white face and miserable eyes. Whatever sort of wound he'd got he was making the most of it, had been the opinion of the man next to me (who had himself got more than he wanted, in both legs). But he must be jolly bad, I thought now, as the Sister came from behind the screen again. His voice went on, in the low rapid, even tone of delerium. Sometimes I could catch what he said, troubled and unhappy and complaining. Someone called Dicky was on his mind, and he kept on crying out to Dicky. 'Don't go out, Dicky; they snipe like hell!' And then, 'Curse the Wood...Dicky, you fool, don't go out!'...All the horror of the Somme attacks was in that raving; all the darkness and the dreadful daylight...I watched the Sister come back with a white-coated doctor the screen glowed comfortingly; soon the disquieting voice became inaudible and I fell asleep. Next morning the screens had vanished the bed was empty, and ready for someone else.

The Home Front 1917

By 1917 very little of the 1914 spirit remained. There was still no guarantee of Allied victory—indeed 1917 stands out as one of the bleakest years of the war. The Revolution in Russia, and the subsequent withdrawal of the Russian armies, allowed additional German forces to be concentrated in France for an all-out attack on the British and French armies; it was at this point that Haig issued his famous 'Backs to the wall' order and, indeed, Britain had her back to the wall in more ways than one.

The glories by 1917 had long passed, along with most of the starry illusions of 1914. Those had been the days when men had volunteered in overwhelming numbers (now they were conscripted), days of the exciting spy-mania, when one child had pleaded about her family's old German house-servant, 'Mummy, must we kill poor Fraulein?', when bands had played daily in the streets, when women had rushed by the millions into any kind of war work, when flags had everywhere fluttered. Then it was that excited girls thrust white feathers at young men who failed to join up quickly, and the newspapers had published that splendid recruiting song, 'Your King and Country Need You':

> Oh, we don't want to lose you,
> But we think you ought to go;
> For your King and your Country
> Both need you so.
> We shall want you and miss you,
> But with all our might and main,
> We will thank you, cheer you, kiss you,
> When you come back again.

By 1917 the novelty of war had gone, and in its place came a new concern for the people, and attempted restriction of even the most basic freedoms, which, as it turned out, Britain said it was fighting for.

Most British people of democratic views had become dismayed by the Defence of the Realm Acts, which had generally torpedoed civil liberties and had substituted courts martial for civil law. Any 'reports likely to cause disaffection or alarm' had become an offence. The police and military were given the power to search and inspect any premises at any time, to seize documents or anything else which the military had reason to suspect was being used, or might be used, for subversive purposes. Anyone could be arrested without a warrant. Suspects could be detained by the military police almost indefinitely until they could be dealt with in the normal course of civil jurisdiction. Military boards could force anyone to live or not to live in a specified area. These and other regrettable regulations had reduced most citizens to a paranoid furtiveness. They tended to avoid strangers, to utter nothing critical, and to refrain from reading or listening to anything defeatist or anti-patriotic. In stereotyped phrases they 'backed the war effort'.

What of those who spoke out, and were not afraid to voice their opinion? Some courageous people did not hesitate to speak out, and foremost among these were the conscientious objectors.

One of these was the writer Lytton Strachey, who, though he had been classified physically unfit, preferred to go through the mill as an objector. At the military tribunal he inflated an air cushion to sit on, in protest against the hard benches, an opening gambit which did not endear him to his inquisitors. When the chairman stated the usual preliminary: 'I understand, Mr Strachey, that you have a conscientious objection to war', he replied in his curious falsetto, 'Oh, no—not at all; only to this war'. And to the triumphant stock question: 'Tell me, Mr Strachey, what would you do if you saw a German soldier trying to violate your sister?' he had replied with pious virtue 'I would try to get between them'.

Wilfred Owen

Sassoon influenced several war poets, one of the greatest of whom was Wilfred Owen, who in 1917 was also a patient at Craiglockhart. Unlike Sassoon, but like many of his other poetic contemporaries, Owen missed the Armistice—by one week—killed by machine-gun fire while leading his troops over a canal. (He died at the same age—twenty five—as Keats, whom he greatly admired.)

Owen was not well known at the time of his death, and it was not until 1920 that Sassoon and Osbert Sitwell edited an anthology of his poetry. Not until the 1940s did they circulate in great numbers. Since then Owen's poetry has become more widely known, especially since it was used by Benjamin Britten for the solo arias in 'War Requiem'. In 1963 an American music critic commented that Owen and Britten had become an article of faith among liberally-minded English people.

The 'War Requiem' takes for its first solo 'Anthem for Doomed Youth'—a poem especially apt for musical setting. In it the poet imagines a whole generation slaughtered, and it is the sort of poem, as one critic has remarked, that Brooke might have written had he lived.

> Not in the hands of boys, but in their eyes,
> Shall shine the holy glimmer of good-byes.

Owen also used mythological figures such as Abraham who becomes the symbol of the old man who sacrifices the young one, Isaac, and 'half the seed of Europe, one by one'.

Above all, his poems express pity, a feeling he has had above all others. In 'Strange Meeting' the ghost of the enemy soldier whom he has bayoneted, calling him friend in the world of shades, says that he might otherwise have made a gift to posterity. In the preface for his War Book, Owen insisted:

> Above all this is not concerned with Poetry. The subject of it is War, and the pity of War. The Poetry is in the pity.

In his introduction to Owen's poetry in the 1920 collection, Sassoon said of his friend 'He never wrote his poems (as so many war poets did) to make the effect of a personal gesture. He pitied others; he did not pity himself'.

A Civilian Poet

Laurence Binyon's 'For the Fallen' is always associated with the remembrance ceremonies on Anzac Day, and his lines express very much the feeling of 1918—a new world awaited—the 'war to end all wars' had finished—and now, while remembering those who had given their lives so that others could be free (or at least, that is what people said publicly), the living wanted to get on with life.

> They shall not grow old, as we that are left grow old;
> Age shall not weary them, nor the years condemn.
> At the going down of the sun and in the morning
> We will remember them.

These lines, often associated with the annual remembrance services, have rhythms of the Bible, and also a close resemblance to Ennobarbas' description of Cleopatra in *Antony and Cleopatra* Act II, Scene 3.

> Age cannot wither her, nor custom stale
> Her infinite variety.

Roger McGough's 'On Picnics' (1966) could only have been written by a member of a different generation to that of 1918. His poem is an interesting contrast to the former, representing a viewpoint from fifty years distance by people to whom the war is now very much part of the long gone past.

> At the goingdown of the sun
> and in the morning
> I try to remember them
> but their names are ordinary names
> and their causes are thighbones
> tugged excitedly from the soil
> by frenchchildren
> on picnics.

VITAI LAMPADA

There's a breathless hush in the Close tonight—
    Ten to make and the match to win—
A bumping pitch and a blinding light,
    An hour to play and the last man in.
And it's not for the sake of a ribboned coat,
    Or the selfish hope of a season's fame,
But his Captain's hand on his shoulder smote:
    'Play up! play up! and play the game!'

The sand of the desert is sodden red,—
    Red with the wreck of a square that broke;—
The Gatling's jammed and the Colonel dead,
    And the regiment blind with dust and smoke,
The river of death has brimmed his banks,
    And England's far, and Honour a name,
But the voice of a schoolboy rallies the ranks:
    'Play up! play up! and play the game!'

This is the word that year by year,
    While in her place the School is set,
Every one of her sons must hear,
    And none that hears it dare forget.
This they all with a joyful mind,
    Beat through life like torch in flame,
And falling fling to the host behind—
    'Play up! play up! and play the game!'

Henry Newbolt

DRUMMER HODGE

They throw in Drummer Hodge, to rest
    Uncoffined—just as found:
His landmark is a kopje—crest
    That breaks the veldt around;
And foreign constellations west
    Each night above his mound.

Young Hodge the Drummer never knew—
    Fresh from his Wessex home—
The meaning of the broad Karoo,
    The bush, the dusty loam,
And why uprose to nightly view
    Strange stars amid the gloam.

Yet portion of that unknown plain
    Will Hodge forever be;
His homely Northern breast and brain
    Grow to some Southern tree,
And strange-eyed constellations reign
    His stars eternally.

(*Thomas Hardy*

From THE FOURTH OF AUGUST

Now in thy splendor go before us,
Spirit of England, ardent-eyed,
Enkindle this dear earth that bore us,
In the hour of peril purified.

The cares we hugged drop out of vision,
Our hearts with thoughts dilate.
We step from days of sour division
Into the grandeur of our fate.

Laurence Binyon

From **MEN WHO MARCH AWAY**

In our heart of hearts believing
   Victory crowns the just,
   And that braggarts must,
   Surely bite the dust,
Press we to the field ungrieving,
In our heart of hearts believing
   Victory crowns the just.

Hence the faith and fire within us
   Men who march away
   Ere the barn-cocks say
   Night is growing gray,
Leaving all that here can win us;
Hence the faith and fire within us
   Men who march away.

Thomas Hardy
(September 1914)

THE OLD SOLDIERS

We come from dock and shipyard, we come from car and train,
We come from foreign countries to slope our arms again,
And, forming fours by numbers or turning to the right,
We're learning all our drill again and 'tis a pretty sight.

Our names are all unspoken, our regiments forgotten,
For some of us were pretty bad and some of us were rotten;
And some will misremember what once they learnt with pain
And hit a bloody sergeant and go to clink again.

Edward Shanks
(1914)

THE DESERTER

'I'm sorry I done it, Major.'
We bandaged the livid face;
And led him out, ere the wan sun rose,
To die his death of disgrace.

The bolt-heads locked to the cartridge;
The rifles steadied to rest,
As cold stock nestled at colder cheek
And foresight lined on the breast.

'Fire!' called the Sergeant-Major.
The muzzles flamed as he spoke:
And the shameless soul of a nameless man
Went up in cordite-smoke.

Gilbert Frankau

THE DEAD

Blow out, you bugles, over the rich Dead!
   There's none of these so lonely and poor of old,
   But, dying, has made us rarer gifts than gold.
These laid the world away; poured out the red
Sweet wine of youth; gave up the years to be
   Of work and joy, and that unhoped serene,
   That men call age; and those who would have been,
Their sons, they gave, their immortality.

Blow, bugles, blow! They brought us, for our dearth,
   Holiness, lacked so long, and Love, and Pain,
Honour has come back, as a king, to earth,
   And paid his subjects with a royal wage;
And nobleness walks in our ways again;
   And we have come into our heritage.

Rupert Brooke

PEACE

Now, God be thanked Who has matched us with His hour,
    And caught our youth, and wakened us from sleeping,
With hand made sure, clear eye, and sharpened power,
    To turn, as swimmers into cleanness leaping,
Glad from a world grown old and cold and weary,
    Leave the sick hearts that honour could not move,
And half-men, and their dirty songs and dreary,
    And all the emptiness of love!

Oh! we, who have known shame, we have found release there,
    Where there's no ill, no grief, but sleep has mending,
    Naught broken save this body, lost but breath;
Nothing to shake the laughing heart's long peace there
    But only agony, and that has ending;
    And the worst friend and enemy is but Death.

Rupert Brooke

THE SOLDIER

If I should die, think only this of me:
    That there's some corner of a foreign field
That is for ever England. There shall be
    In that rich earth a richer dust concealed;
A dust whom England bore, shaped, made aware,
    Gave, once, her flowers to love, her ways to roam,
A body of England's, breathing English air,
    Washed by the rivers, blest by suns of home.

And think, this heart, all evil shed away,
    A pulse in the eternal mind, no less
      Gives somewhere back the thoughts by England given;
Her sights and sounds; dreams happy as her day;
    And laughter, learnt of friends; and gentleness,
    In hearts at peace, under an English heaven.

Rupert Brooke
(Died en-route to Gallipoli, 1915)

ENGLAND TO HER SONS

Sons of mine, I hear you thrilling
To the trumpet call of war;
Gird ye then, I give you freely
As I gave your sires before,
All the noblest of the children I in love and anguish bore.

Free in service, wise in justice,
Fearing but dishonour's breath;
Steeled to suffer uncomplaining,
Loss and failure, pain and death;
Strong in faith that sees the issue and in hope that triumpheth.

Go, and may the God of battles
You in His good guidance keep;
And if He in wisdom giveth
Unto His beloved sleep,
I accept it, nothing asking, save a little space to weep.

W.N. Hodgson

COMMON FORM

If any question why we died,
Tell them because our fathers lied.

Rudyard Kipling

TWO FUSILIERS

And what have we done with War at last?
Well, we've been lucky devils both,
And there's no need of pledge or oath
To bind our lovely friendship fast,
By firmer stuff
Close bound enough.

By wire and wood and stake we're bound,
By Fribourt and Festubert,
By whipping rain, by the sun's glare,
By all the misery and loud sound,
By a Spring day,
By Picard clay.

Show me the two so closely bound
As we, by the wet bond of blood,
By friendship blossoming from mud,
By Death: we faced him, and we found
Beauty in Death,
In dead men, breath.

Robert Graves

IN FLANDERS FIELDS

In Flanders fields the poppies blow
Between the crosses, row on row
    That mark our place; and in the sky
    The larks, still bravely singing, fly
Scarce heard amid the guns below.

We are the Dead. Short days ago
We lived, felt dawn, saw sunset glow,
    Loved and were loved, and now we lie
        In Flanders fields.

Take up our quarrel with the foe:
To you from failing hands we throw
    The torch; be yours to hold it high.
    If ye break faith with us who die
We shall not sleep, though poppies grow
        In Flanders fields.

John McRae
(died in Base Hospital, 1918)

A DEAD STATESMAN

I could not dig: I dared not rob:
Therefore I lied to please the mob.
Now all my lies are proved untrue
And I must face the men I slew.
What tale shall serve me here among
Mine angry and defrauded young?

Rudyard Kipling

RENDEZVOUS

I have a rendezvous with Death
At some disputed barricade,
When Spring comes back with rustling shade
And apple-blossoms fill the air—
I have a rendezvous with Death
When Spring brings back blue days and fair.

It may be he shall take my hand
And lead me into his dark land
And close my eyes and quench my breath—
It may be I shall pass him still.
I have a rendezvous with Death
On some scarred slope of battered hill,
When Spring comes round again this year
And the first meadow-flowers appear.

God knows 'twere better to be deep
Pillowed in silk and scented down,
Where love throbs out in blissful sleep,
Pulse nigh to pulse, and breath to breath,
Where hushed awakenings are dear . . .
But I've a rendezvous with Death
At midnight in some flaming town,
When Spring trips north again this year,
And I to my pledged word am true,
I shall not fail that rendezvous.

Alan Seeger
(killed in action, 1916)

FLANDERS

Man has the life of butterflies
In the sunshine of sacrifice;
Brief and brilliant, but more
Guerdon than the honeyed flower,
And more glory than the grace
Of their gentle floating pace.

Willoughby Weaving

BOMBARDMENT

Four days the earth was rent and torn
By bursting steel,
The houses fell about us;
Three nights we dared not sleep,
Sweating, and listening for the imminent crash
Which meant our death.

The fourth night every man,
Nerve-tortured, racked to exhaustion,
Slept, muttering and twitching,
While the shells crashed overhead.

The fifth day there came a hush;
We left our holes
And looked above the wreckage of the earth
To where the white clouds moved in silent lines
Across the untroubled blue.

Richard Aldington

HOW LONG, O LORD?

How long, O Lord, how long, before the flood
Of crimson-welling carnage shall abate?
From sodden plains in West and East the blood
Of kindly men streams up in mists of hate,
Polluting Thy clean air: and nations great
In reputation of the arts that bind
The world with hopes of Heaven, sink to the state
Of brute barbarians, whose ferocious mind
Gloats o'er the bloody havoc of their kind,
Not knowing love or mercy. Lord, how long
Shall Satan in high places lead the blind
To battle for the passions of the strong?
Oh, touch Thy children's hearts, that they may know
Hate their most hateful, pride deadliest foe.

Robert Palmer
(killed in action, 1916)

THE DYING SOLDIER

'Here are the houses,' he moaned,
'I could reach, but my brain swims.'
Then they thundered and flashed,
And shook the earth to its rims.

'They are gunpits,' he gasped,
'Our men are at the guns.
Water!... Water!... Oh, water!
For one of England's dying sons.'

'We cannot give you water,
Were all England in your breath.'
'Water!... Water!... Oh, water!'
He moaned and swooned to death.

Isaac Rosenberg
(killed in action, 1918)

TRENCH POETS

I knew a man, he was my chum,
but he grew blacker every day,
and would not brush the flies away,
nor blanch however fierce the hum
of passing shells; I used to read,
to rouse him, random things from Donne—
like 'Get with child a mandrake-root.'
But you can tell he was far gone,
for he lay gaping, mackerel-eyed,
and stiff and senseless as a post
even when that old poet cried
'I long to talk with some old lover's ghost.'

I tried the Elegies one day,
but he, because he heard me say:
'What needst thou have more covering than a man?'
grinned nastily, and so I knew
the worms had got his brains at last.
There was one thing that I might do
To starve the worms; I racked my head
for healthy things and quoted *Maud*.
His grin got worse and I could see
he sneered at passion's purity.
He stank so badly, though we were great chums
I had to leave him; then rats ate his thumbs.

Edgell Rickword

THE TARGET

I shot him, and it had to be
One of us! Twas him or me.
'Couldn't be helped,' and none can blame
Me for you would do the same.

My mother, she can't sleep for fear
Of what might be a-happening here
To me. Perhaps it might be best
To die and set her fears at rest.

For worst is worst, and worry's done
Perhaps he was the only son...
Yet God keeps still, and does not say
A word of Guidance any way.

Well, if they get me first, I'll find
That boy, and tell him all my mind,
And see who felt the bullet worst,
And ask his pardon, if I durst.

All's a tangle, here's my job.
A man might rave, or shout, or sob;
And God He takes no sort of heed.
This is a bloody mess indeed.

Ivor Gurney

UNKNOWN FEMALE CORPSE

Headless, lacking foot and hand,
Horrible I come to land.
I beseech all women's sons
Know I was a mother once.

Rudyard Kipling

SOLILOQUY I

No, I'm not afraid of death
(Not very much afraid, that is)
Either for others or myself;
Can watch them coming from the line
On the wheeled silent stretchers
And not shrink,
But munch my sandwich stoically
And make a joke when 'it' has passed.

But—the way they wobble!—
God! that makes one sick.
Dead men should be so still, austere,
And beautiful,
Not wobbling carrion roped upon a cart...

Well, thank God for rum.

Richard Aldington

SOLILOQUY II

I was wrong, quite wrong;
The dead men are not always carrion.
After the advance,
As we went through the shattered trenches
Which the enemy had left,
We found, lying upon the fire-step,
A dead English soldier,
His head bloodily bandaged
And his closed left hand touching the earth,

More beautiful than one can tell,
More subtly coloured than a perfect Goya,
And more austere and lovely in repose
Than Angelo's hand could ever carve in stone.

Richard Aldington

A SHELL

Here we are all, naked as Greeks,
Killing the lice in our shirts:
Suddenly the air is torn asunder,
Ripped as coarse silk,
Then a dull thud...
We are all squatting.

Frederic Manning

THE FACE

Out of the smoke of men's wrath,
The red mist of anger,
Suddenly,
As a wraith of sleep,
A boy's face, white and tense,
Convulsed with terror and hate,
The lips trembling...

Then a red smear, falling...
I thrust aside the cloud, as it were tangible,
Blinded with a mist of blood,
The face cometh again
As a wraith of sleep:
A boy's face delicate and blonde,
The very mask of God,
Broken.

Frederic Manning

THE LEVELLER

Near Martinpuisch that night of hell
Two men were struck by the same shell,
Together tumbling in one heap
Senseless and limp like slaughtered sheep.

One was a pale eighteen-year-old,
Girlish and thin and not too bold,
Pressed for the war ten years too soon,
The shame and pity of his platoon.

The other came from far-off lands
With bristling chin and whiskered hands,
He had known death and hell before
In Mexico and Ecuador.

Yet in his death this cut-throat wild
Groaned 'Mother! Mother!' like a child,
While that poor innocent in man's clothes
Died cursing God with brutal oaths.

Old Sergeant Smith, kindest of men,
Wrote out two copies there and then
Of his accustomed funeral speech.
To cheer the womenfolk of each.

He died a hero's death and we
His comrades of 'A' Company
Send heartfelt sympathies, we shall
All greatly miss so true a pal.

Robert Graves

DIED OF WOUNDS

His wet white face and miserable eyes
Brought nurses to him more than groans and sighs:
But hoarse and low and rapid rose and fell
His troubled voice: he did the business well.

The ward grew dark; but he was still complaining
And calling out for 'Dickie'. 'Curse the Wood.'
It's time to go. O Christ, and what's the good?
We'll never take it, and it's always raining.'

I wondered where he'd been; then heard him shout,
'They snipe like hell! O Dickie, don't go out'...
I fell asleep... Next morning he was dead;
And some Slight Wound lay smiling on his bed.

Siegfried Sassoon

BASE DETAILS

If I were fierce, and bald, and short of breath,
  I'd live with scarlet Majors at the Base,
And speed glum heroes up the line to death.
  You'd see me with my puffy petulant face,
Guzzling and gulping in the best hotel,
  Reading the Roll of Honour. 'Poor young chap,'
I'd say—'I used to know his father well;
  Yes, we've lost heavily in this last scrap.'
And when the war is done and youth stone dead,
  I'd toddle safely home and die—in bed.

Siegfried Sassoon

AFTER THE BATTLE

So they are satisfied with our Brigade,
  And it remains to parcel out the bays!
And we shall have the usual Thanks Parade,
  The beaming General, and the soapy praise.

You will come up in your capricious car
  To find your heroes sulking in the rain,
To tell us how magnificent we are,
  And how you hope we'll do the same again.

And we, who knew your old abusive tongue,
  Who heard you hector us a week before,
We who have bled to boost you up a rung—
  A K.C.B. perhaps, perhaps a Corps—

We who must mourn these spaces in the mess,
  And somehow fill those hollows in the heart,
We do not want your Sermon in Success,
  Your greasy benisons on Being Smart.

We only want to take our wounds away.
  To some warm village where the tumult ends,
And drowsing in the sunshine many a day,
  Forget our aches, forget that we had friends.

Weary we are of blood and noise and pain;
  This was a week we shall not soon forget;
And if, indeed, we have to fight again,
  We little wish to think about it yet.

We have done well; we like to hear it said.
  Say it, and then, for God's sake, say no more.
Fight, if you must, fresh battles far ahead,
  But keep them dark behind your chateau door!

A.P. Herbert

BREAKFAST

We ate our breakfast lying on our backs
Because the shells were screeching overhead.
I bet a rasher to a loaf of bread
That Hull United would beat Halifax
When Jimmy Stainthorpe played full-back instead
Of Billy Bradford. Ginger raised his head
And cursed, and took the bet, and dropped back dead.
We ate our breakfast lying on our backs
Because the shells were screeching overhead.

Wilfrid Gibson

'BLIGHTERS'

The House is crammed: tier beyond tier they grin
And cackle at the Show, while prancing ranks
Of harlots shrill the chorus, drunk with din;
'We're sure the Kaiser loves our dear old Tanks!'

I'd like to see a Tank come down the stalls,
Lurching to rag-time tunes, or 'Home, sweet Home',
And there'd be no more jokes in Music-halls
To mock the riddled corpses round Bapaume.

Siegfried Sassoon

THE DUG-OUT

Why do you lie with your legs ungainly huddled,
And one arm bent across your sullen, cold,
Exhausted face? It hurts my heart to watch you,
Deep-shadow'd from the candle's guttering gold;
And you wonder why I shake you by the shoulder;
Drowsy, you mumble and sigh and turn your head...
You are too young to fall asleep for ever;
And when you sleep you remind me of the dead.

Siegfried Sassoon

LAMENTATIONS

I found him in the guard-room at the Base.
From the blind darkness I had heard his crying
And blundered in. With puzzled, patient face
A sergeant watched him; it is no good trying
To stop it; for he howled and beat his chest.
And, all because his brother had gone west,
Raved at the bleeding war; his rampant grief
Moaned, shouted, sobbed, and choked, while he was kneeling
Half-naked on the floor. In my belief
Such men have lost all patriotic feeling.

Siegfried Sassoon

A PRIVATE

This ploughman dead in battle slept out of doors
Many a frozen night, and merrily
Answered staid drinkers, good bedmen, and all bores:
'At Mrs Greenland's Hawthorn Bush', said he,
'I slept.' None knew which bush. Above the town,
Beyond 'The Drover', a hundred spot the down
In Wiltshire. And where now at last he sleeps
More sound in France—that, too, he secret keeps.

Edward Thomas

THE FAVOUR

Death favoured me from the first, well knowing I could not
 endure
To wait on him day by day. He quitted my betters and
 came
Whistling over the fields, and, when he had made all sure,
 'Thy line is at an end,' he said, 'but at least I have saved
 its name.'

Rudyard Kipling

From GOLD BRAID

Same old trenches, same old view,
   Same old rats as blooming tame,
Same old dug-outs, nothing new,
   Same old smell, the very same,
Same old bodies out in front,
   Same old strafe from two till four,
Same old scratching, same old 'unt,
   Same old bloody war.

A.A. Milne

THE NEXT WAR

War's a joke for me and you,
While we know such dreams are true.
    Siegfried Sassoon

Out there, we've walked quite friendly up to Death;
   Sat down and eaten with him, cool and bland,
   Pardoned his spilling mess-tins in our hand.
We've sniffed the green thick odour of his breath—
Our eyes wept, but our courage didn't writhe.
   He's spat at us with bullets and he's coughed
   Shrapnel. We chorussed when he sang aloft;
We whistled while he shaved us with his scythe.

Oh, Death was never enemy of ours!
   We laughed at him, we leagued with him, old chum.
No soldier's paid to kick against his powers.
   We laughed, knowing that better men would come,
And greater wars; when each proud fighter brags
He wars on Death—for lives; not men—for flags.

Wilfred Owen

THE PARABLE OF THE OLD MAN AND THE YOUNG

So Abram rose, and clave the wood, and went,
And took the fire with him, and a knife.
And as they sojourned both of them together,
Isaac the first-born spake and said, My Father,
Behold the preparations, fire and iron,
But where the lamb for this burnt-offering?
Then Abram bound the youth with belts and straps,
And builded parapets and trenches there,
And stretched forth the knife to slay his son.
When lo! an angel called him out of heaven,
Saying, Lay not thy hand upon the lad,
Neither do anything to him. Behold,
A ram, caught in a thicket by its horns;
Offer the Ram of Pride instead of him.
But the old man would not so, but slew his son,
And half the seed of Europe, one by one.

Wilfred Owen

FUTILITY

Move him into the sun—
Gently its touch awoke him once,
At home, whispering of fields unsown.
Always it woke him, even in France,
Until this morning and this snow.
If anything might rouse him now
The kind old sun will know.

Think how it wakes the seeds,—
Woke, once, the clays of a cold star.
Are limbs, so dear-achieved, are sides,
Full-nerved—still warm—too hard to stir?
Was it for this the clay grew tall?
—O what made fatuous sunbeams toil
To break earth's sleep at all?

Wilfred Owen

DOES IT MATTER ?

Does it matter?—losing your legs?...
For people will always be kind,
And you need not show that you mind
When others come in after hunting
To gobble their muffins and eggs.

Does it matter?—losing your sight?...
There's such splendid work for the blind;
And people will always be kind,
As you sit on the terrace remembering
And turning your face to the light.

Do they matter?—those dreams from the pit?...
You can drink and forget and be glad,
And people won't say that you're mad,
For they'll know you've fought for your country
And no one will worry a bit.

Siegfried Sassoon

DREAMERS

Soldiers are citizens of death's gray land,
    Drawing no dividends from time's tomorrows.
In the great hour of destiny they stand,
    Each with his feuds, and jealousies, and sorrows.
Soldiers are sworn to action, they must win
    Some flaming, fatal climax with their lives.
Soldiers are dreamers; when the guns begin
    They think of firelit homes, clean beds, and wives.

I see them in foul dugouts, gnawed by rats,
    And in the ruined trenches, lashed with rain,
Dreaming of things they did with balls and bats,
    And mocked with hopeless longing to regain
Bank holidays, and picture shows, and spats,
    And going to the office in the train.

Siegfried Sassoon

A. E. F.

There will be a rusty gun on the wall, sweetheart,
The rifle grooves curling with flakes of rust.
A spider will make a silver string nest in the darkest warmest
    corner of it.
The trigger and the range-finder, they too will be rusty.
And no hands will polish the gun, and it will hang on the wall
Forefingers and thumbs will point absently and casually toward it
It will be spoken among half-forgotten, wished-to-be-forgotten
    things.
They will tell the spider: Go on, you're doing good work.

Carl Sandburg

THE GENERAL

'Good-morning; good-morning!' the General said
When we met him last week on our way to the line.
Now the soldiers he smiled at are most of 'em dead,
And we're cursing his staff for incompetent swine.
'He's a cheery old card', grunted Harry to Jack
As they slogged up to Arras with rifle and pack.
But he did for them both by his plan of attack.

Siegfried Sassoon

FIVE SOULS

First Soul

I was a peasant of the Polish plain;
I left my plough because the message ran:—
Russia in danger, needed every man
To save her from the Teuton; and was slain.
I gave my life for freedom—This I know
For those who bade me fight had told me so.

Second Soul

I was a Tyrolese, a mountaineer;
I gladly left my mountain home to fight
Against the brutal treacherous Muscovite;
And died in Poland on a Cossack spear.
I gave my life for freedom—This I know
For those who bade me fight had told me so.

Third Soul

I worked in Lyons at my weaver's loom,
When suddenly the Prussian despot hurled
His felon blow at France and at the world;
Then I went forth to Belgium and my doom.
I gave my life for freedom—This I know
For those who bade me fight had told me so.

Fourth Soul

I owned a vineyard by the wooded Main,
Until the Fatherland begirt by foes
Lusting her downfall, called me, and I rose
Swift to the call—and died in far Lorraine.
I gave my life for freedom—This I know
For those who bade me fight had told me so.

Fifth Soul

I worked in a great shipyard by the Clyde;
There came a sudden word of wars declared,
Of Belgium, peaceful, helpless, unprepared,
Asking our aid: I joined the ranks, and died.
I gave my life for freedom—This I know
For those who bade me fight had told me so.

W.N. Ewer

THE BAYONET

This bloody steel
Has killed a man.
I heard him squeal
As on I ran.

He watched me come
With wagging head.
I pressed it home,
And he was dead.

Though clean and clear
I've wiped the steel,
I still can hear
That dying squeal.

Wilfrid Gibson

BOMBED IN LONDON

On land and sea I strove with anxious care
To escape conscription. It was in the air!

Rudyard Kipling

A SON

My son was killed while laughing at some jest. I would I knew
What it was, and it might serve me in time when jests are few.

Rudyard Kipling

YPRES

With a dull and hazy light
  the sun of a winter noon
    swills
      thy ruins,
Thy ruins etched
  in silver silhouettes
    against a turquoise sky.
Lank poles leap to the infinite,
  their broken wires
    tossed like the rat-locks of Maenades.
And Desolation broods over all,
  gathering to her lap
    her leprous children.
The sparrows whimper
  amid the broken arches.

Herbert Read

POISON

Forget, and forgive them—you say:
  War's bitterness passes;
Wild rose wreaths the gun-pit today,
  Where the trench was, young grass is;
    Forget and forgive:
    Let them live.

Forgive them—you say—and forget;
  Since struggle is finished,
Shake hands, be at peace, square the debt,
  Let old hates be diminished;
    Abandon blockade,
    Let them trade.

Fools! Shall the pard change his skin
  Or cleanse one spot from it?
As the lecher returns to his sin
  So the cur to his vomit.
    Fools! Hath the Hun
    Earned place in the sun?

You who accuse that I fan
  War's spark from hate's ember,
Forgive and forget if you can;
  But, I, I remember
    Men who faced death
    Choking for breath.

Four years back to a day—
  Men who fought cleanly.
Killed say you? Murdered, *I* say,
  Murdered, most meanly,
    Poisoned!...And yet,
    You can forget.

Gilbert Frankau

(21 April 1919—four years after the introduction
of poisonous gas by the Germans at Ypres)

ANTHEM FOR DOOMED YOUTH

What passing-bells for these who die as cattle?
   Only the monstrous anger of the guns.
   Only the stuttering rifles' rapid rattle
Can patter out their hasty orisons.
No mockeries now for them; nor prayers nor bells,
   Nor any voice of mourning save the choirs,—
The shrill demented choirs of wailing shells;
   And bugles calling for them from sad shires.

What candles may be held to speed them all?
   Not in the hands of boys, but in their eyes
Shall shine the holy glimmers of good-byes.
   The pallor of girls' brows shall be their pall;
Their flowers the tenderness of patient minds,
And each slow dusk a drawing-down of blinds.

Wilfred Owen

AT A CALVARY NEAR THE ANCRE

One ever hangs where shelled roads part.
   In this war He too lost a limb,
But His disciples hide apart;
   And now the soldiers bear with Him.

Near Golgotha strolls many a priest,
   And on their faces there is pride
That they were flesh-marked by the Beast
   By whom the gentle Christ's denied.

The scribes on all the people shove
   And bawl allegiance to the state,
But they who love the greater love
   Lay down their life; they do not hate.

Wilfred Owen

THE SEND-OFF

Down the close, darkening lanes they sang their way
To the siding-shed,
And lined the train with faces grimly gay.

Their breasts were struck all white with wreath and spray
As men's are, dead.

Dull porters watched them, and a casual tramp
Stood staring hard,
Sorry to miss them from the upland camp.
Then, unmoved, signals nodded, and a lamp
Winked to the guard.

So secretly, like wrongs hushed-up, they went.
They were not ours:
We never heard to which front these were sent.

Nor there if they yet mock what women meant
Who gave them flowers.

Shall they return to beatings of great bells
In wild train-loads?
A few, a few, too few for drums and yells,
May creep back, silent, to still village wells
Up half-known roads.

Wilfred Owen

STRANGE MEETING

It seemed that out of battle I escaped
Down some profound dull tunnel, long since scooped
Through granite which titanic wars had groined.
Yet also there encumbered sleepers groaned,
Too fast in thought or death to be bestirred.
Then, as I probed them, one sprang up, and stared
With piteous recognition in fixed eyes,
Lifting distressful hands as if to bless.
And by his smile, I knew that sullen hall,
By his dead smile I knew we stood in Hell.
With a thousand pains that vision's face was grained;
Yet no blood reached there from the upper ground,
And no guns thumped, or down the flues made moan.
'Strange friend,' I said, 'here is no cause to mourn.'
'None,' said the other, 'save the undone years,
The hopelessness. Whatever hope is yours,
Was my life also; I went hunting wild
After the wildest beauty in the world,
Which lies not calm in eyes, or braided hair,
But mocks the steady running of the hour,
And if it grieves, grieves richlier than here.
For of my glee might many men have laughed,
And of my weeping something had been left,
Which must die now. I mean the truth untold,
The pity of war, the pity war distilled.
Now men will go content with what we spoiled.
Or, discontent, boil bloody, and be spilled.
They will be swift with swiftness of the tigress.
None will break ranks, though nations trek from progress,
Courage was mine, and I had mystery,
Wisdom was mine, and I had mastery:
To miss the march of this retreating world
Into vain citadels that are not walled.

Then, when much blood had clogged their chariot-wheels,
I would go up and wash them from sweet wells,
Even with truths that lie too deep for taint.
I would have poured my spirit without stint
But not through wounds; not on the cess of war.
Foreheads of men have bled where no wounds were
I am the enemy you killed, my friend.
I knew you in this dark: for so you frowned
Yesterday through me as you jabbed and killed.
I parried; but my hands were loath and cold.
Let us sleep now...'

Wilfred Owen
(found among his papers)

ATTACK

At dawn the ridge emerges massed and dun
In the wild purple of the glow'ring sun,
Smoldering through spouts of drifting smoke that shroud
The menacing scarred slope; and, one by one,
Tanks creep and topple forward to the wire.
The barrage roars and lifts. Then, clumsily bowed
With bombs and gun and shovels and battle-gear,
Men jostle and climb to meet the bristling fire.
Lines of grey, muttering faces, masked with fear,
They leave their trenches, going over the top,
While time ticks blank and busy on their wrists,
And hope, with furtive eyes and grappling fists,
Flounders in mud. O Jesus, make it stop!

Siegfried Sassoon

FOR THE FALLEN

With proud thanksgiving, a mother for her children,
England mourns for her dead across the sea.
Flesh of her flesh they were, spirit of her spirit,
Fallen in the cause of the free.

Solemn the drums thrill; Death august and royal
Sings sorrow up into immortal spheres,
There is music in the midst of desolation
And a glory that shines upon our tears.

They went with songs to the battle, they were young,
Straight of limb, true of eye, steady and aglow.
They were staunch to the end against odds uncounted:
They fell with their faces to the foe.

They shall grow not old as we that are left grow old:
Age shall not weary them, nor the years condemn.
At the going down of the sun and in the morning
We will remember them.

They mingle not with their laughing comrades again;
They sit no more at familiar tables at home;
They have no lot in our labour of the day-time:
They sleep beyond England's foam.

But where our desires are and our hopes profound,
Felt as a well-spring that is hidden from sight,
To the innermost heart of their own land they are known
As the stars are known to the Night;

As the stars that shall be bright when they are dust,
Moving in marches upon the heavenly plain;
As the stars that are starry in the time of our darkness,
To the end, to the end, they remain.

Laurence Binyon

DULCE ET DECORUM EST

Bent double, like old beggars under sacks,
Knock-kneed, coughing like hags, we cursed through sludge,
Till on the haunting flares we turned our backs
And towards our distant rest began to trudge.
Men marched asleep. Many had lost their boots
But limped on, blood-shod. All went lame; all blind;
Drunk with fatigue; deaf even to the hoots
Of tired, outstripped Five-Nines that dropped behind.

Gas! GAS! Quick, boys!—An ecstasy of fumbling,
Fitting the clumsy helmets just in time;
But someone still was yelling out and stumbling
And flound' ring like a man in fire or lime . . .
Dim, through the misty panes and thick green light,
As under a green sea, I saw him drowning.

In all my dreams, before my helpless sight,
He plunges at me, guttering, choking, drowning.
If in some smothering dreams you too could pace
Behind the wagon that we flung him in,
And watch the white eyes writhing in his face,
His hanging face, like a devil's sick of sin;
If you could hear, at every jolt, the blood
Come gargling from the froth-corrupted lungs,
Obscene as cancer, bitter as the cud
Of vile, incurable sores on innocent tongues,—
My friend, you would not tell with such high zest
To children ardent for some desperate glory,
The old Lie: Dulce et decorum est
Pro patria mori.

Wilfred Owen

AFTERMATH

Have you forgotten yet?...
For the world's events have rumbled on since those gagged days,
Like traffic checked at the crossing of city-ways:
And the haunted gap in your mind has filled with thoughts that flow
Like clouds in the lit heaven of life; and you're a man reprieved to go,
Taking your peaceful share of Time, with joy to spare.
But the past is just the same—and War's a bloody game...
Have you forgotten yet?...
Look down, and swear by the slain of the War that you'll never forget.

Do you remember the dark months you held the sector at Mametz—
The nights you watched and wired and dug and piled sandbags on
    parapets?
Do you remember the rats; and the stench
Of corpses rotting in the front-line trench—
And dawn coming, dirty-white, and chill with a hopeless rain?
Do you ever stop and ask, 'Is it all going to happen again?'

Do you remember that hour of din before the attack—
And the anger, the blind compassion that seized and shook you then
As you peered at the doomed and haggard faces of your men?
Do you remember the stretcher-cases lurching back
With dying eyes and lolling heads—those ashen-grey
Masks of the lads who once were keen and kind and gay?

Have you forgotten yet?...
Look up, and swear by the green of the spring that you'll never forget.

Siegfried Sassoon
(March 1919)

THIS GENERATION

Their youth was fevered—passionate, quick to drain
    The last few pleasures from the cup of life
Before they turned to suck the dregs of pain
    And end their young-old lives in mortal strife.
They paid the debts of many a hundred year
    Of foolishness and riches in alloy.
They went to death; nor did they shed a tear
    For all they sacrificed of love and joy.
Their tears ran dry when they were in the womb,
For, entering life—they found it was their tomb.

Osbert Sitwell

From HOW SHALL WE RISE TO GREET THE DAWN.

Continually they cackle thus,
These venerable birds,
Crying, 'Those whom the Gods love
Die young'
Or something of that sort.

Osbert Sitwell

NIGHTFALL

Hooded in angry mist, the sun goes down:
Steel-gray the clouds roll out across the sea:
Is this a Kingdom? Then give Death the crown,
For here no emperor hath won, save He.

Herbert Asquith
(Sanctury Wood, 1917)

HIGH WOOD

Ladies and gentlemen, this is High Wood,
Called by the French, Bois des Fourneaux,
The famous spot which in Nineteen-Sixteen,
July, August and September was the scene
Of long and bitterly contested strife,
By reason of its High commanding site.
Observe the effect of shell-fire in the trees
Standing and fallen; here is wire; this trench
For months inhabited, twelve times changed hands;
(They soon fall in), used later as a grave.
It has been said on good authority
That in the fighting for this patch of wood
Were killed somewhere above eight thousand men,
Of whom the greater part were buried here,
This mound on which you stand being...
      Madame, please,
You are requested kindly not to touch
Or take away the Company's property
As souvenirs; you'll find we have on sale
A large variety, all guaranteed.
As I was saying, all is as it was,
This is an unknown British officer,
The tunic having lately rotted off.
Please follow me—this way...
      the path, sir, please,
The ground which was secured at great expense
The Company keeps absolutely untouched,
And in that dug-out (genuine) we provide
Refreshments at a reasonable rate.
You are requested not to leave about
Paper, or ginger-beer bottles, or orange peel,
There are waste-paper baskets at the gate.

Philip Johnstone
(1918)

TWELVE MONTHS AFTER

Hullo! here's my platoon, the lot I had last year.
'The war'll be over soon.'
  'What 'opes?'
    'No bloody fear!'
Then 'Number Seven, 'shun! All present and correct.'
They're standing in the sun, impassive and erect.
Young Gibson with his grin; and Morgan, tired and white;
Jordan, who's out to win a D.C.M. some night;
And Hughes that's keen on wiring; and Davies ('79),
Who always must be firing at the Boche front line.

       *   *   **

'Old soldiers never die; they simply fide a-why!'
That's what they used to sing along the roads last spring;
That's what they used to say before the push began;
That's where they are today, knocked over to a man.

Siegfried Sassoon

DEATH

Nor dread nor hope attend
A dying animal;
A man awaits his end
Dreading and hoping all;
Many times he died,
Many times rose again.
A great man in his pride
Confronting murderous men
Casts derision upon
Supersession of breath;
He knows death to the bone—
Man has created death.

W.B. Yeats

Part II THE LOST PEACE 1919-1939

Background

The period between the wars saw many threats to world peace, especially in the decade of the thirties. Some of the great ideological and political issues of the century arose in this decade—fascism, communism and liberal democracy, pacifism and militarism, moral traditionalism and progressivism all of which were debated passionately, sometimes resulting in battles in the streets such as those in Germany between Communists and National Socialists, and in the East End of London between the Communists and Sir Oswald Mosley's Black Shirts.

In retrospect the 1930s were the prelude to war, although naturally this was not so obvious then. (When Winston Churchill, seeing what lay ahead, called for rearmament in 1932 he was labelled a war-monger.) The Depression had thrown the economic system of the West out of gear and, as it slowly recovered, the international situation deteriorated in counter balance—a process beginning with the Japanese invasion of Manchuria in 1931, and culminating in the German invasion of Poland in 1939.

The Spanish Civil War

1936 stands as a turning point in the inter-war years. In July began the Spanish Civil War, the most traumatic and bloody conflict since the Great War, and one which, before it was over, would lead to the death of over a million soldiers and civilians.

Britain and France refused to help either side, and adopted a policy of non-intervention—which unwittingly helped General Franco and his Nationalists who were receiving help from Germany and Italy. (For a time, the loyalists received almost no aid whatsoever.)

Salvation of sorts came to the loyalist forces from the Soviet Union which shrewdly refused aid until the Communist Party was given control of the Republican effort. Out of this arose the disillusionment with Communism, which culminated for most with the Soviet-German Non-Agression Pact in 1939—though not for a few till the Hungarian Uprising in 1956.

Many poets and intellectuals had heralded the war in a manner similar to that of the 'Salad Days' of 1914—but in Spain too the war dragged on until any romantic flavour which once may have existed was truly buried. The Communists appeared more anxious to destroy the Anarchists and Trotskyites than the Fascists and it became clear that, far from being a struggle for democratic liberties, the civil war had become a useful military training ground for the Axis powers, and a great propaganda platform for the Soviet Union.

Reaction to the War

In the initial fervour for the war, many people whose views favoured the Left became war minded, saying the dictators had to be stopped before they became stronger, while those whose sympathies lay on the Right supported a non-intervention policy.

The war too quickly caught the imagination of the poets, many of whom joined the International Brigade to help the Republicans. H.W. Auden worked for a time as a stretcher bearer, while Spender was head of English broadcasting in a Spanish radio station.

It is interesting to note that Roy Campbell was the only poet of any merit to express fascist sympathies and fight on Franco's side, although Ezra Pound (living in Italy) expressed strong fascist sympathies.

As did the Great War, the Spanish blood-bath led to the death of promising poets, and brilliant young men like John Cornford, Julian Bell, Ralph Fox, and the great Spanish poet, Garcia Lorca, were killed before their talents had time to fully develop.

As with Vietnam today, groups appeared expressing concern over the war. The Friends of Spain favoured the Republicans—the Friends of Nationalist Spain favoured Franco, while the press was about equally divided.

Broadly speaking, Spain was to the generation of the 1930s what Vietnam has become to that of the 1960s. The anti-war movement followed similar lines—thousands signed the Peace Pledge Union, vowing never to fight a war.

The feelings aroused by the conflict in Spain, can be profitably compared with feelings today over issues such as Biafra, Vietnam, or the Middle East.

One of the most popular novels to come out of the war was Hemingway's *For Whom the Bell Tolls*—an interesting account of the life (and death) of an American teacher—Robert Jordan—fighting with Loyalist guerilla forces. (Hemingway was a reporter for the American Newspaper Alliance in Madrid during the war.)

The title of the novel is significant. What Donne said in Meditation 17 applies just as much today, if not more so, as it did in the seventeenth century:

No man is an Island, entire of itself; every man is a piece of the Continent, a part of the main; if a Clod be washed away by the Sea Europe is the less, as well as if a Manor of thy friends or of thine own were; any man's death diminishes me, because I am involved in Mankind; and therefore never send to know for whom the bell tolls;

It tolls for thee.

From JOURNEY TO A WAR 1939

XII

Here war is harmless like a monument:
A telephone is talking to a man;
Flags on a map declare that troops were sent;
A boy brings milk in bowls. There is a plan

For living men in terror of their lives,
Who thirst at nine who were to thirst at noon,
Who can be lost and are, who miss their wives
And, unlike an idea, can die too soon.

Yet ideas can be true, although men die:
For we have seen a myriad faces
Estatic from one lie,

And maps can really point to places
Where life is evil now,
Nanking. Dachau.

W.H. Auden

CHRIST IN UNIFORM

Close at my side a girl and boy
Fell firing, in the doorway here,
Collapsing with a strangled cheer
As on the very couch of joy,
And onward through a wall of fire
A thousand others rolled the surge,
And where a dozen men expire
A thousand myrmidons emerge—
As if the Christ, our Solar Sire,
Magnificent in their intent,
Returned the bloody way he went,
Of so much blood, of such desire,
And so much valour proudly spent,
To weld a single heart of fire.

Roy Campbell

From OVERTURES TO DEATH 1938

Newsreel

Enter the dream-house, brothers and sisters, leaving
Your debts asleep, your history at the door:
This is the home for heroes, and this loving
Darkness a fur you can afford.

Fish in their tank electrically heated
Nose without envy the glass wall: for them
Clerk, spy, nurse, killer, prince, the great and the deaf defeated,
Move in a mute day-dream.

Bathed in this common source, you gape incurious
At what your active hours have willed—
Sleep-walking on that silver wall, the furious
Sick shapes and pregnant fancies of your world.

There is the mayor opening the oyster season:
A society wedding: the autumn hats look swell:
An old crocks' race, and a politician
In fishing-waders to prove that all is well.

Oh, look at the warplanes! Screaming hysteric treble
In the low power-dive, like gannets they fall steep.
But what are they to trouble—
These silver shadows to trouble your watery, womb-deep sleep?

See the big guns, rising, groping, erected
To plant death in your world's soft womb.
Fire-bud, smoke-blossom, iron seed projected—
Are these exotics? They will grow nearer home:

Grow nearer home—and out of the dream-house stumbling
One night into a strangling air and the flung
Rags of children and thunder of stone niagaras tumbling
You'll know you slept too long.

C. Day Lewis

FULL MOON AT TIERZ:
BEFORE THE STORMING OF HUESCA

The past, a glacier, gripped the mountain wall,
And time was inches, dark was all.
But here it scales the end of the range,
The dialectic's point of change,
Crashes in light and minutes to its fall.
Time present is a cataract whose force
Breaks down the banks even at its source
And history forming in our hands
Not plasticine but roaring sands,
Yet we must swing it to its final course.

The intersecting lines that cross both ways,
Time future, has no image in space,
Crooked as the road that we must tread,
Straight as our bullets fly ahead.
We are the future. The last fight let us face.

John Cornford
(killed in action, Cordoba, 1936)

DO NOT GO GENTLE INTO THAT GOOD NIGHT

Do not go gentle into that good night,
Old age should burn and rave at close of day;
Rage, rage against the dying of the light.

Though wise men at their end know dark is right,
Because their words had forked no lightning they
Do not go gentle into that good night.

Good men, the last wave by, crying how bright
Their frail deeds might have danced in a green bay,
Rage, rage against the dying of the light.

Wild men who caught and sang the sun in flight,
And learn, too late, they grieved it on its way,
Do not go gentle into that good night.

Grave men, near death, who see with blinding sight
Blind eyes could blaze like meteors and be gay,
Rage, rage against the dying of the light.

And you, my father, there on the sad height,
Curse, bless, me now with your fierce tears, I pray.
Do not go gentle into that good night.
Rage, rage against the dying of the light.

Dylan Thomas

AND DEATH SHALL HAVE NO DOMINION

And death shall have no dominion.
Dead men naked they shall be one
With the man in the wind and the west moon;
When their bones are picked clean and the clean bones gone,
They shall have stars at elbow and foot;
Though they go mad they shall be sane,
Though they sink through the sea they shall rise again;
Though lovers be lost love shall not;
And death shall have no dominion.

And death shall have no dominion.
Under the windings of the sea
They lying long shall not die windily;
Twisting on racks when sinews give way,
Strapped to a wheel, yet they shall not break;
Faith in their hands shall snap in two,
And the unicorn evils run them through;
Split all ends up they shan't crack;
And death shall have no dominion.

And death shall have no dominion.
No more may gulls cry at their ears
Or waves break loud on the seashores;
Where blew a flower may a flower no more
Lift its head to the blows of the rain;
Though they be mad and dead as nails,
Heads of the characters hammer through daisies;
Break in the sun till the sun breaks down,
And death shall have no dominion.

Dylan Thomas

THE HAND THAT SIGNED THE PAPER

The hand that signed the paper felled a city;
Five sovereign fingers taxed the breath,
Doubled the globe of dead and halved a country;
These five kings did a king to death.

The mighty hand leads to a sloping shoulder,
The finger-joints are cramped with chalk;
A goose's quill has put an end to murder
That put an end to talk.

The hand that signed the treaty bred a fever,
And famine grew, and locusts came;
Great is the hand that holds dominion over
Man by a scribbled name.

The five kings count the dead but do not soften
The crusted wound nor stroke the brow;
A hand rules pity as a hand rules heaven;
Hands have no tears to flow.

Dylan Thomas

From **THE HEART'S JOURNEY**
XXI

ON PASSING THE NEW MENIN GATE

Who will remember, passing through this Gate,
The unheroic Dead who fed the guns?
Who shall absolve the foulness of their fate,—
Those doomed, conscripted, unvictorious ones?
Crudely renewed, the Salient holds its own.
Paid are its dim defenders by this pomp;
Paid, with a pile of peace-complacent stone,
The armies who endured that sullen swamp.

Here was the world's worst wound. And here with pride
'Their name liveth for ever,' the Gateway claims.
Was ever an immolation so belied
As these intolerably nameless names?
  Well might the Dead who struggled in the slime
  Rise and deride this sepulchre of crime.

Siegfried Sassoon

WORDS ASLEEP

Now I am still and spent
and lie in a whited sepulchre
breathing dead

but there will be
no lifting of the damp swathes
no return of blood
no rolling away the stone

till the cocks carve sharp
gild scars in the morning
and carry the stirring sun
and the early dust to my ears.

Laurie Lee
(Andalucia, 1936)

A LETTER FROM ARAGON

This is a quiet sector of a quiet front.

We buried Ruiz in a new pine coffin,
But the shroud was too small and his washed feet stuck out.
The stink of corpse came through the clean pine boards
And some of the bearers wrapped handkerchiefs round their faces
Death was not dignified.
We hacked a ragged grave in the unfriendly earth
And fired a ragged volley over the grave.

You could tell from our listnessess, no one much missed him.

This is a quiet sector of a quiet front.
There is no poison gas and no H.E.

But when they shelled the other end of the village
And the streets were choked with dust
Women came screaming out of the crumbling houses,
Clutched under one arm the naked rump of an infant.
I thought: how ugly fear is.

This is a quiet sector of a quiet front.
Our nerves are steady; we all sleep soundly.

In the clean hospital bed my eyes were so heavy
Sleep easily blotted out one ugly picture,
A wounded militiaman moaning in a stretcher,
Now out of danger, but still crying for water
Strong against death, but unprepared for such pain.

This is a quiet front.

But when I shook hands to leave, an Anarchist worker
Said: 'Tell the workers of England
This was a war not of our own making,
We did not seek it.
But if ever the Fascists again rule Barcelona
It will be as a heap of ruins with us workers beneath it.'

John Cornford
(1936)

FALL OF A CITY

All the posters on the walls
All the leaflets in the streets
Are mutilated, destroyed or run in the rain,
Their words blotted out with tears,
Skins peeling from their bodies
In the victorious hurricane.

All the names of heroes in the hall
Where the feet thundered and the bronze throats roared,
FOX and LORCA claimed as history on the walls,
Are now angrily deleted
Or to dust surrender their dust,
From golden praise excluded.

All the badges and salutes
Torn from lapels and from hands
Are thrown away with human sacks they wore
Or in the deepest bed of mind
They are washed over with a smile
Which launches the victors when they win.

All the lessons learned, unlearnt;
The young, who learned to read, now blind
Their eyes with archaic film;
The peasant relapses to a stumbling tune
Following the donkey's bray;
These only remember to forget.

But somewhere some word presses
On the high door of a skull, and in some corner
Of an irrefrangible eye
Some old man's memory jumps to a child
—Spark from the days of energy.
And the child hoards it like a bitter toy.

Stephen Spender

BOMBING CASUALTIES IN SPAIN

Dolls' faces are rosier but these were children
their eyes not glass but gleaming gristle
dark lenses in whose quicksilvery glances
the sunlight quivered. These blench'd lips
were warm once and bright with blood
but blood
held in a moist blob of flesh
not spilt and spatter'd in tousled hair.

In these shadowy tresses
red petals did not always
thus clot and blacken to a scar.
These are dead faces.
Wasp's nests are not more wanly waxen
wood embers not so greyly ashen.

They are laid out in ranks
like paper lanterns that have fallen
after a night of riot
extinct in the dry morning air.

Herbert Read

REFUGEE BLUES

Say this city has ten million souls,
Some are living in mansions, some are living in holes:
Yet there's no place for us, my dear, yet there's no place for us.

Once we had a country and we thought we had it fair,
Look in the atlas and you'll find it there:
We cannot go there now, my dear, we cannot go there now.

In the village churchyard there grows an old yew,
Every spring it blossoms anew:
Old passports can't do that, my dear, old passports can't do that.

The consul banged the table and said;
'If you've got no passport, you're officially dead':
But we are still alive, my dear, we are still alive.

Went to a committee; they offered me a chair;
Asked me politely to return next year:
But where shall we go to-day, my dear, but where shall we go today?

Came to a public meeting; the speaker got up and said:
'If we let them in, they will steal our daily bread';
He was talking of you and me, my dear, he was talking of you and me.

Thought I heard the thunder rumbling in the sky;
It was Hitler over Europe, saying: 'They must die';
O we were in his mind, my dear, O we were in his mind.

Saw a poodle in a jacket fastened with a pin,
Saw a door opened and a cat let in:
But they weren't German Jews, my dear, but they weren't German Jews.

Went down the harbour and stood upon the quay,
Saw the fish swimming as if they were free:
Only ten feet away, my dear, only ten feet away.

Walked through a wood, saw the birds in the trees;
They had no politicians and sang at their ease:
They weren't the human race, my dear, they weren't the human race.

Dreamed I saw a building with a thousand floors,
A thousand windows and a thousand doors;
Not one of them was ours, my dear, not one of them was ours.

Stood on a great plain in the falling snow;
Ten thousand soldiers marched to and fro:
Looking for you and me, my dear, looking for you and me.

W.H. Auden

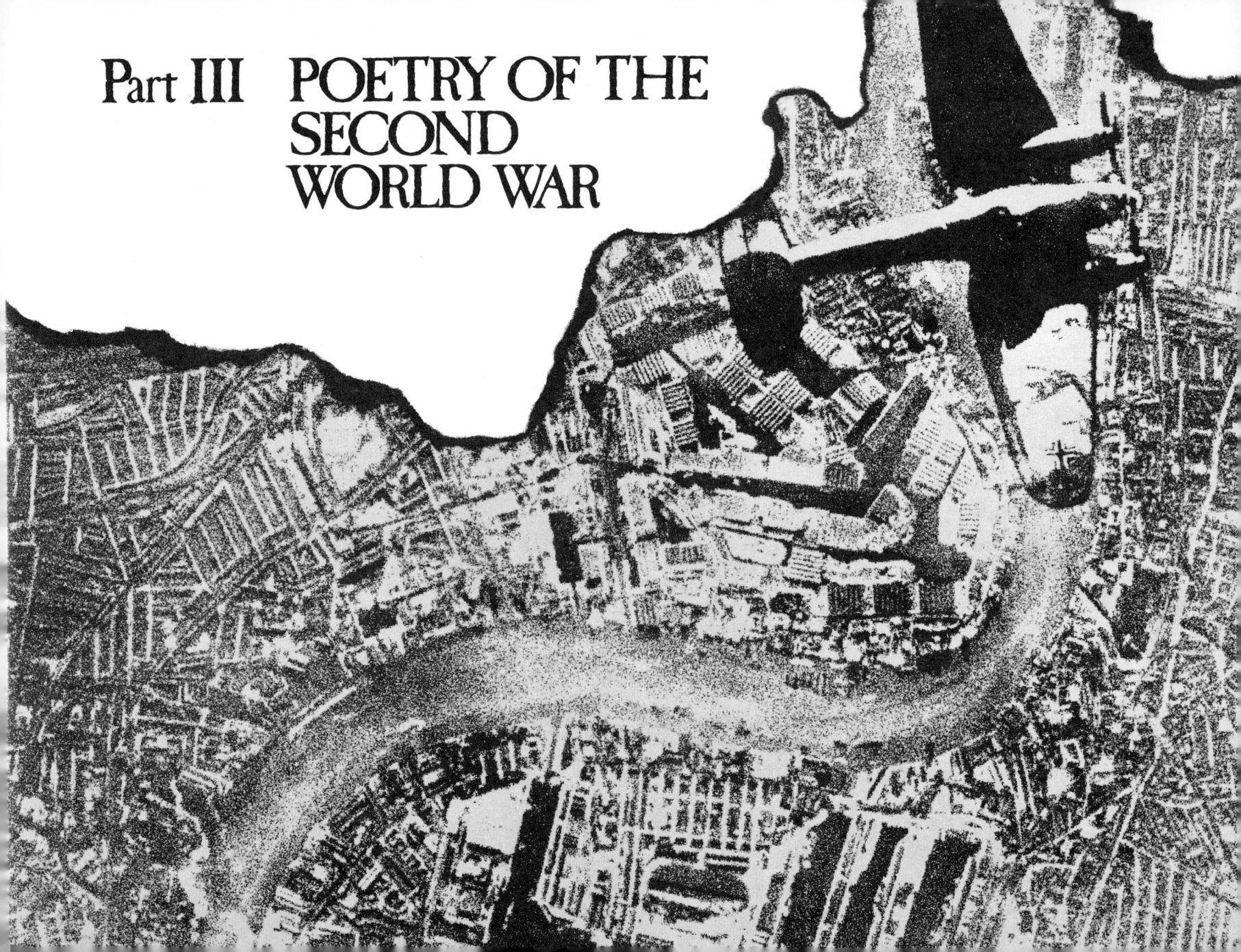

Part III POETRY OF THE SECOND WORLD WAR

For the second time in the lives of most of us we are at war. Over and over again we have tried to find a peaceful way out of the differences between ourselves and those who are now our enemies. But it has been in vain. We have been forced into a conflict. For we are called with our allies, to meet the challenge of a principle which, if it were to prevail, would be fatal to any civilized order in the world.

Broadcast, 3 September 1939. H.M. King George VI

Background

To many people, poetry of the Second World War is valueless when compared to that of the Great War. The war produced no Owens, Sassoons or Rosenbergs—a fact which critics explain by contending that none of sufficient talent emerged in this period. It is, however, undeniable that a number of good poems were written, even if they did not receive the public applause given those of the earlier generation. As in the Great War and the Spanish Civil War, a number of the poets were killed—some of the greatest of the Second World War poets died before the end of the war. Alan Lewis was killed in 1944 and Keith Douglas, the Second World War poet who stands nearest in succession to Wilfred Owen, was killed in the same year. Sydney Keyes, the most prolific of the Second World War poets, was not quite twenty-one when he died in action in North Africa in 1943. To many, Keyes began where Wilfred Owen left off. 'If the word that Wilfred Owen made his own was "pity", Keyes' word is "pain"', wrote R.N. Currey, adding, 'Keyes' work is a continuation of Wilfred Owen's'. Together with Douglas, Keyes shares the greatest promise of all the poets of this generation.

From the start, there was less idealism in 1939. In 1914 major war was something which England had not experienced for generations, while in 1939 the Great War was still fresh in memory, and the threat of Fascism was real enough to dispel any illusions which people may have had. As Anthony Burgess says in *The Novel Now*:

> The First World War produced many works of great merit... but the Hitler war failed to produce poets of the calibre of Siegfried Sassoon and Wilfred Owen. Perhaps it was

because the stamping out of a wretched tyranny was a necessary grim chore, and guiltily belated one; it could not stimulate the imagination with that at least initial crusading fervour which fired Rupert Brooke in 1914. Moreover the First World War was to become so useless and wasteful that all that writers came to see in it was purely mythical—the old men cold-bloodedly destroying the young—and the poets and novelists welcome myth, however ghastly. But the later war only stimulated the desire to keep records—usually of the universal experience of boredom followed by danger—and record keeping rarely becomes an art.

The New Poetry

The war poets of the Second World War were slow at first in appearing—'Where are the war-poets?' asked the *Times Literary Supplement* in 1940. The press asked the same question also, with patriotic indignation. Before long there were accusations—it was implied that, while everybody else had taken up their action stations, the poets had not—and they who had been so noisy about Spain!

Some poets took a pessimistic view of Britain's chances, and had left for safer and brighter pastures. W.H. Auden was in America, an act which caused great offence in Britain and one which was not purged by the logic of E.M. Forster's remark that it was better to be a swimming rat than a sinking ship. Auden had no need to apologise; like Churchill he had been warning of the dangers of fascism a whole decade before Neville Chamberlain came on the air on 3 September 1939.

Conscription was introduced at the start of the war in 1939, and not halfway through as it was in 1916. In 1939 the concepts of warfare had changed, and many of the men of superior education—the potential poets—were drafted into strategic, educational, intelligence, and even civil service work instead of being sent to the front. This had the effect of preserving their lives but it also prevented them from viewing battle at first hand, and experiencing the shock of front-line action, which had so activated the earlier war poets.

The purpose of much of the poetry of the earlier war was to communicate; to let the people know what was happening. The radio, the newsreel, the direct report from the battlefield, were not possible in 1914–18, and the poets and correspondents played an important part in informing the public of events. This was not so in 1939 when radio, newsreel, and press provided plentiful information.

Europe and the Blitz

The experience of war in 1940 was different too. After the period of the Phoney War, Allied forces quickly collapsed, France fell to the German forces, while the B.E.F. only just managed to escape from Dunkirk. By the end of 1940 Europe from Norway to France was in German hands. At this stage Churchill became Prime Minister, and the Luftwaffe began its Blitz on Britain.

> I have nothing to offer but blood, toil, tears and sweat. . . . We have before us an ordeal of the most grievous kind. . . You ask, what is our policy? I will say: It is to wage war, by sea, land and air, with all our might and with all the strength that God can give us; to wage war against a monstrous tyranny, never surpassed in the dark, lamentable catalogue of human crime.
>
> Broadcast, 13 May 1940

Not since the days of William the Conqueror had Britain been so dangerously close to invasion and defeat:

> Let us therefore brace ourselves to our duty, and so bear ourselves that if the British Empire and Commonwealth lasts for a thousand years men will still say: 'This was their finest hour'.
>
> Broadcast, 5 June 1940

It was a period when the danger was greater than when the Spanish Armada threatened the freedom of the 'island race' and Churchill, soldier, war-correspondent, historian and politician, quickly found an apt historical reference;

> It [the week when possibility of invasion was greatest] ranks with the days when the Spanish Armada was approaching the Channel, and Drake was finishing his game of bowls; or when Nelson stood between us and Napoleon's Grand Army at Boulogne. We have read all about this in the history books; but what is happening now is on a far greater scale and of far more consequence to the life and future of the world and its civilization than those brave old days.
>
> Broadcast, 11 September 1940

It was now as dangerous to live in London or Coventry as it was to be 'somewhere in France' or 'somewhere in North Africa'. Civilians came to understand better just what war now meant;

> When I married my Bert 'e made a little little 'ome for me. Vawses on the mantelpiece, a gramophone in the corner, everything pretty. When 'e went away to the Army, I kept worrying lest the Germans should come and bomb it. Kept on worrying, you know! Then two nights ago they came and bombed it, so now there's nothing to worry about. See?
>
> October 1940.
>
> A scrubbing maid at Charing Cross Hospital. (Quoted in Sir Philip Gibbs' *The Pageant of the Years*.)

No civilian poet in 1940 or 1941 would emulate the pathetically comic 'Air Raid: 1917–18' by Herbert Palmer:

> I wonder if they'll come tonight!
> The round moon rolls in silvery light,
> No sound throbs on the windless air.
>
> For, though I tremble to confess,
> I never feel more cheerfulness
> Than when the German raiders fly
> Like bees across the cloudless sky.

With the bombing raids all night and most of the day in 1940, it was difficult to remain cheerful. T.S. Eliot wrote of the bombing in

'Little Gidding'; while Edith Sitwell in 'Still Falls the Rain' produced a profoundly moving poem in which she is seen as a mourner at the crucifixion of cities during air-raids: However, it was Dylan Thomas who translated statistics into loss, in 'A child of a few hours', and 'A man aged a hundred'.

The Air

> Never in the field of human conflict, has so much been
> owed by so many, to so few.
>
> Broadcast, 20 August 1940

The use of air power was fully realised in this war—the military use of aircraft transformed the scope of war, widening its geographical boundaries almost without limit. With this, came a new kind of poet, the air-force poet, inspired by the solitude one often felt in the air. John Corby and John Pudney became well known for their verse, as did Randall Jarrell, whose 'Death of the Ball Turret Gunner' illustrates the extreme dangers faced by airmen each time they went aloft:

> From my mother's sleep I fell into the State,
> And I hunched in its belly till my wet fur froze.
> Six miles from earth, loosed from its dream of life,
> I woke to black flak and the nightmare fighters.
> When I died they washed me out of the turret with a hose.

(The ball turret gunner was in one of the most dangerous positions in the giant B-29 'Superfortress' bomber—the gun position in the exposed underbelly of the plane. It is often said by ex-airmen that there were few if any atheists on a bombing mission. Certainly they suffered high casualties, especially in the rear gunner position in the 'Lancasters' of the R.A.F., and the ball turret gunner position in the 'Superfortresses' of the U.S.A.A.F.)

The New Technology

Technology always advances at a faster pace during time of war than in peace time, and 1939–45 was no exception—it began with small bombing raids, graduated to the giant thousand bomber raids over Germany, and eventually reached a climax with the bombing of Hiroshima and Nagasaki. This technology at first interested many poets—the use of various machines, radios, and new gadgets developed a new language based on jargon, half-formed words, abbreviations, and codes, expressed in Henry Reed's 'Naming of Parts', Ian Serraillier's 'The New Learning' and David Bourne's 'Operations calling'.

Radio was an important link in the desert tank battles, as well as at sea and in the air. Keith Douglas in *Alamein* described a battle conducted entirely by radio-telephone:

> The heavy tanks are engaging targets on the ridge in front of us, behind which we can see the tops of telegraph poles. Every turn of events is recorded on the air. Someone asks for 'the little fat man'—this means they are hopelessly broken down and want the technical adjutant, known officially over the wireless as 'Tock Ack', to arrange their recovery. The regiment on our right asks for 'our bald-headed friends' on such occasions. It is these individual peculiarities which an enemy listening officer will note. The armoured cars in front, 'Our red friends on ponies, the Cherry Ps', wheel away towards the regiment on our right—'Uncle Gordon's boys'. Now and then an awkward, hesitating transmission creates a short silence—'Nuts three calling. We 'ave, er 'ad a misfortune. The horse 'as fallen, driver is no more. Can we have Monkey Orange?' The gunner of a tank which has been hit, shaken by the impact of the shell, the sight of one of his friends beheaded, and another bleeding from a great wound, has forgotten his wireless procedure, if he ever knew it. If the M.O. is not already attending to someone, he will try to reach the tank in a scout car. Meanwhile, the gunner must try to get the unconscious corporal out, because the tank is burning, and bandage him roughly, because he is bleeding to death.

Unfortunately technology did not remove the tragedy of war—it was still a business in which people were liable to die. The new technology made war more widespread, brought civilians into the front lines and, as was gradually revealed after January 1945, enabled the German conquerors in Europe to efficiently carry out their plan for the 'final solution' which shortly shocked the world.

We shall have failed, and blood of our dearest will have flowed in vain, if the victory which they died to win does not lead to a lasting peace, founded on justice and goodwill. To that, then let us turn our thoughts, on this day of just triumph and proud sorrow; and then take up our work again, resolved as a people to do nothing unworthy of those who died for us, and to make the world such a world as they would have desired for their children and for ours.

Broadcast, 8 May 1945. H.M. King George VI

THE RECRUIT

Pried from the circle where his family ends,
Man on his own, no hero of old tales,
Discovers when the pose of lone wolf fails
Loneliness and, miraculously, friends.

Finds how his comradeship with one depends
On being both from London, say, or Wales,
How with the next a common job prevails,
Sport with a third, and so the list extends.

Nation and region, class and craft and syndicate
Are only some: all attributes connect
Their owner with his kind, call him to vindicate

A common honour; and his self-respect
Starts from the moment when his senses indicate
'I' as a point where circles intersect.

John Manifold

THE NEW LEARNING

With hatred now all lips and wings
the human mind does silly things.
Common sense has fled, and reason
is definitely out of season.

In nature class the schoolboy's head
is taught to contemplate, instead
of flower pot and cactus stump,
a budding aluminium dump.

Can God that made the cactus grow
do miracles he wants to know?
Can He that made the water wine
make Spitfires of a pot and pan?

He knows that, loving human life,
God strongly disapproves of strife
and doesn't care a damn for guns
except if they are British ones.

'The British blockade will bring salvation'
(he's told) 'to every neutral nation.
So starve them! then, their lands restored,
they'll all be free to praise the Lord.

'You think the Bible's right—it ain't
now that a murderer's a saint.
The new commandment's "Thou shalt kill
in order to effect God's will".'

And so with tanks for people's toes
the Christian soldier onward goes.

Ian Serraillier

TELL US THE TRICKS

Say, soldier! Tell us the tricks,
   the tackle of your trade;
The passage of your hours;
   the plans that you have made—
Of what do you think—what consider?
Tell us of the slow process,
That gradual change
   from man to soldier—?

And what can I say, what reply?
   There is no answer.
The tale is hidden in the eye.
The soldier's here—the man is not:
Man's voice was lost;
The sex decayed
By the bitter bayonet—the chattering shot
The growth delayed.
The brief days of youth,
And its forgotten past,
Cannot be commanded to appear,
We hope they may last
   —some other time—some different year.

Paul Scott

FOR JOHNNY

Do not despair
For Johnny-head-in-air;
He sleeps as sound
As Johnny underground.

Fetch out no shroud
For Johnny-in-the-cloud;
And keep your tears
For him in after years.

Better by far
For Johnny-the-bright-star,
To keep your head,
And see his children fed.

John Pudney

MISSING

Less said the better.
The bill unpaid, the dead letter.
No roses at the end
Of Smith, my friend.

Last words don't matter,
And there are none to flatter.
Words will not fill the post
Of Smith, the ghost.

For Smith, our brother,
Only son of loving mother,
The ocean lifted, stirred,
Leaving no word.

John Pudney

REPORTED MISSING

With broken wing they limped across the sky
caught in late sunlight, with their gunner dead,
one engine gone, —the type was out-of-date,—
blood on the fuselage turning brown from red:

knew it was finished, looking at the sea
which shone back patterns in kaleidoscope
knew that their shadow would meet them by the way,
close and catch at them, drown their single hope:

sat in this tattered scarecrow of the sky
hearing it cough, the great plane catching
now the first dark clouds upon her wing-base,—
patching the great tear in evening mockery.

So two men waited, saw the third dead face,
and wondered when the wind would let them die.

John Bayliss

AIR GUNNER

The eye behind this gun made peace
With a boy's eye which doubted, trembled,
Guileless in the mocking light
Of frontiers where death assembled.

Peace was as single as the dawn,
Flew straightly as the birds migrating,
Timelessly in tune with time,
Purposeful, uncalculating.

So boyish doubt was put away:
The man's eye and the boy's were one.
Mockery and death retreat
Before the eye behind this gun.

John Pudney

COMBAT REPORT

Just then I saw the bloody Hun.
You saw the Hun? You, light and easy,
Carving the soundless daylight. I was breezy
When I saw that Hun. Oh wonder
Pattern of stress, of nerve poise, flyer,
Overtaking time. He came out under
Nine-tenths cloud, but I was higher.
Did Michelangelo aspire,
Painting and laughing cumulus, to ride
The majesty of air. He was a trier
I'll give him that, the Hun. So you convert
Ultimate sky to airspeed, drift, and cover:
Sure with the tricky tools of God and lover.
I let him have a sharp four-second squirt,
Closing to fifty yards. He went on fire.
Your deadly petals painted, you exert
A simple stature. Man-high, without pride,
You pick your way through heaven and the dirt.
He burnt out in the air: that's how the poor sod died.

John Pudney

WAR

When the bloom is off the garden,
and I'm fighting in the sky,
when the lawns and flower beds harden,
and when weak birds starve and die,
and death-roll will grow longer,
eyes will be moist and red;
and the more I will kill, the longer
shall I miss friends who are dead.

Nigel Weir
(killed in action, 1940)

'OPERATIONS CALLING!'

'Clearing Black Section
Patrol Bass Rock,'
Leaps heart; after shock
Action comes stumbling;
Snatch your helmet;
Then run smoothly, to the grumbling
Of a dozen Merlin heating
Supercharged air,
You are there
By' 'Z'.

Down hard on the behind
The parachute; you are blind
With your oxygen snout
But click, click, click, click, you feel
And the harness is fixed.
Round the wing
And 'Out of the cockpit, you,'
Clamber the rung
And the wing as if a wasp had stung
You, hop and jump into the cockpit,
Split second to spike
The Sutton harness holes,
One, two, three, four,
Thrust with your
Hand to the throttle open...

'Operations' called and spoken.

David Bourne
(killed in action, 1941)

CORVETTE

Dully she shudders at the solid water
A pause, and spray stings angrily over.
She plunges, and the noisy foam leaps widely
Marbling the moon-grey sea. Loud in the shrouds
Untrammelled wind roar songs of liberty.
Free as the petrels hovering astern
Her long lithe body answers to the swell.

Pardon if all the cleaness and the beauty
Brave rhythm and the immemorial sea
Ensnare us sometimes with their siren song,
Forgetful of our murderous intentions.
Through our uneasy peacetime carnival
Cold sweat of death rained on us like a dew;
Even this grey machinery of murder
Holds beauty and the promise of a future.

Norman Hampson
(H.M.S. *Carnation*, 1942)

ACTION STATIONS

'Action stations.' Tin hats and apprehension;
Rush to guns and hoses, engine room
And wireless office. Air of tension.
Eyes uplifted and some seawards gazing.
Ears are strained for a distant 'boom',
Or roar of engines. Lips are phrasing
Prayers, maybe, or curse upon the Hun.
Friendly aircraft in the distance loom
And are gone. Minutes pass...'Carry On'.

John Wedge

DESTROYERS IN THE ARCTIC

Camouflaged, they detach lengths of sea and sky
When they move; offset, speed and direction are a lie.

Everything is grey anyway; ships, water, snow, faces.
Flanking the convoy, we rarely go through our paces.

But sometimes on tightening waves at night they wheel
Drawing white moons on strings from dripping keel.

Cold cases them, like ships in glass; they are formal,
Not real, except in adversity. Then, too, have to seem normal.

At dusk they intensify dusk, strung out, non-commital:
Waves spill from our wake, crepe paper magnetised by gun-metal.

They breathe silence, less solid than ghosts, ruminative
As the Arctic breaks up on their sides and they sieve

Moisture into mess-decks. Heat is cold-lined here,
Where we wait for a torpedo and lack air.

Repetitive of each other, imitating the sea's lift and fall,
On the wings of the convoy they indicate rehearsal.

Merchantmen move sideways, with the gait of crustaceans,
Round whom like eels escorts take up their stations.

Landfall, Murmansk; but starboard now a lead-coloured
Island, Jan Mayen. Days identical, hoisted like sails, blurred.

Counters moved on an Admiralty map—snow like confetti
Covers the real us. We dream we are counterfeits tied to our jetty.

But cannot dream long; the sea curdles and sprawls,
Liverishly real, and merciless all else away from us falls.

Alan Ross

SONG OF THE DYING GUNNER

Oh mother my mouth is full of stars
As cartridges in the tray
My blood is a twin-branched scarlet tree
And it runs all runs away.

Oh Cooks to the Galley is sounded off
And the lads are down in the mess
But I lie done by the forrard gun
With a bullet in my breast.

Don't send me a parcel at Christmas time
Of socks and nutty and wine
And don't depend on a long weekend
By the Great Western Railway line.

Farewell, Aggie Weston, the Barracks at Guz,
Hang my tiddley suit on the door
I'm sewn up neat in a canvas sheet
And I shan't be home no more.

Charles Causley
(on H.M.S. *Glory*)

A WAR

There set out, slowly, for a Different World,
At four, on winter mornings, different legs . . .
You can't break eggs without making an omelette
—That's what they tell the eggs.

Randall Jarrell

NAVAL BASE

Waiting in the bar for the war to end—
Those who for the second time saw it begin
And, charting the future, watched death crawling
Like a lizard over the lidless eyes of the sun
And the leprous face of the coast being eaten
Away by the sea—the glass shows them now
The face and features that they find appalling.
Reflections of launches move across the mirror,
Detroyers and corvettes swinging round buoys, sweepers
At anchor—but here the voyages begin and end,
Gin-time stories which they hear, like keepers
Of lightships, as they wait for news of friends—
The same routine, continuing the war until it ends.

Alan Ross

POEM

We in our haste can only see the small components of the scene
We cannot tell what incidents will focus on the final screen.
A barrage of disruptive sound, a petal on a sleeping face,
Both must be noted, both must have their place;
It may be that our later selves or else our unborn sons
Will search for meaning in the dust of long deserted guns,
We only watch, and indicate and make our scribbling pencil
    notes.
We do not wish to moralize, only to ease our dusty throats.

Donald Bain

STILL FALLS THE RAIN

(*The Raids, 1940. Night and Dawn*)

Still falls the Rain—
Dark as the world of man, black as our loss—
Blind as the nineteen hundred and forty nails
Upon the Cross.

Still falls the Rain
With a sound like the pulse of the heart that is changed
  to the hammer-beat
In the Potter's Field, and the sound of the impious feet

On the Tomb:
  Still falls the Rain
In the Field of Blood where the small hopes breed and
  the human brain
Nurtures its greed, that worm with the brow of Cain.

Still falls the Rain
At the feet of the Starved Man hung upon the Cross.
Christ that each day, each night, nails there, have mercy
  on us—
On Dives and on Lazarus:
Under the Rain the sore and the gold are as one.

Still falls the Rain—
Still falls the Blood from the Starved Man's wounded
  Side:
He bears in His Heart all wounds,—those of the light
  that died,
The last faint spark
In the self-murdered heart, the wounds of the sad
  uncomprehending dark,
The wounds of the baited bear,—
The blind and weeping bear whom the keepers beat
On his helpless flesh...the tears of the hunted hare.

Still falls the Rain—
Then—O Ile leape up to my God: who pulles me doune—
See, see where Christ's blood streames in the firmament:
It flows from the Brow we nailed upon the tree
Deep to the dying, to the thirsting heart
That holds the fires of the world,—dark-smirched with
  pain
As Caesar's laurel crown.

Then sounds the voice of One who like the heart of man
Was once a child who among beasts has lain—
'Still do I love, still shed my innocent light, my Blood,
  for thee.'

Edith Sitwell

UNSEEN FIRE

This is a damned inhuman sort of war.
I have been fighting in a dressing-gown
Most of the night; I cannot see the guns,
The sweating gun-detachments or the planes;

I sweat down here before a symbol thrown
Upon a screen, sift facts, initiate
Swift calculations and swift orders; wait
For the precise split-second to order fire.

We chant our ritual words; beyond the phones
A ghost repeats the orders to the guns:
One Fire...Two Fire...ghosts answer: the guns
    roar
Abruptly; and an aircraft waging war
Inhumanly from nearly five miles height
Meets our bouquet of death—and turns sharp right.

                                        R.N. Currey

RURAL RAID

Earth opens where the squandered bombs fall wide
And all our view's a burning countryside.
Each fairy-lamp incendiary that falls
Is like a juggler adding to his balls
Tossing up more, to glitter every colour,
And when one's watched an hour, there's nothing duller.
Only the sudden metal weight of fear
Brings back the platitude that life is dear,
Keeps us awake while we sit staring out
With Reason pounding, 'What's it all about?'.

                                        Denton Welch

A REFUSAL TO MOURN THE DEATH, BY FIRE, OF A CHILD IN LONDON

Never until the mankind making
Bird beast and flower
Father and all humbling darkness
Tells with silence the last light breaking
And the still hour
Is come of the sea tumbling in harness

And I must enter again the round
Zion of the water bead
And the synagogue of the ear of corn
Shall I let pray the shadow of a sound
Or sow my salt seed
In the least valley of sackcloth to mourn

The majesty and burning of the child's death.
I shall not murder
The mankind of her going with a grave truth
Nor blaspheme down the stations of the breath
With any further
Elegy of innocence and youth.

Deep with the first dead lies London's daughter,
Robed in the long friends,
The grains beyond age, the dark veins of her mother,
Secret by the unmourning water
Of the riding Thames.
After the first death, there is no other.

                                        Dylan Thomas

ALL DAY IT HAS RAINED

All day it has rained, and we on the edge of the moors
Have sprawled in our bell-tents, moody and dull as boors,
Groundsheets and blankets spread on the muddy ground
And from the first grey wakening we have found
No refuge from the skirmishing fine rain
And the wind that made the canvas heave and flap
And the taut wet guy-ropes ravel out and snap.
All day the rain has glided, wave and mist and dream,
Drenching the gorse and heather, a gossamer stream
Too light to move the acorns that suddenly
Snatched from their cups by the wild south-westerly
Pattered against the tent and our upturned dreaming faces.
And we stretched out, unbuttoning our braces,
Smoking a Woodbine, darning dirty socks,
Reading the Sunday papers—I saw a fox
And mentioned it in the note I scribbled home;—
And we talked girls, and dropping bombs on Rome,
And thought of the quiet dead and the loud celebrities
Exhorting us to slaughter, and the herded refugees;
—Yet thought softly, morosely of them, and as indifferently
As of ourselves or those whom we
For years have loved, and will again
Tomorrow maybe love; but now it is the rain
Possesses us entirely, the twilight and the rain.

And I can remember nothing dearer or more to my heart
Than the children I watched in the woods on Saturday
Shaking down burning chestnuts for the schoolyard's merry play,
Or the shaggy patient dog who followed me
By Sheet and Steep and up the wooded scree
To the Shoulder o'Mutton where Edward Thomas brooded long
On death and beauty—till a bullet stopped his song.

Alun Lewis

WAR POET

I am the man who looked for peace and found
My own eyes barbed.
I am the man who groped for words and found
An arrow in my hand.
I am the builder whose firm walls surround
A slipping land.
When I grow sick or mad
Mock me not nor chain me:
When I reach for the wind
Cast me not down:
Though my face is a burnt book
And a wasted town.

Sidney Keyes

INSTEAD OF A CAROL

The winter hardens. Every night I hear
The patient, khaki beast grieve in his stall,
His eyes behind the harsh fingers soft as wool.
His cheerful morning face puts me in mind
Of certain things were rumoured far and near
To hearts wherein there fretted and repined
A world that came to its last dated year.

Rayner Heppenstall

SIMPLIFY ME WHEN I'M DEAD

Remember me when I am dead
and simplify me when I'm dead.

As the process of earth
strip off the colour and the skin:
take the brown hair and the blue eye

and leave me simpler than at birth,
when hairless I came howling in
as the moon entered the cold sky.

Of my skeleton perhaps,
so stripped, a learned man will say
'He was of such type and intelligence,' no more.

Thus when in a year collapse
particular memories, you may
deduce, from the long pain I bore
the opinions I held, who was my foe

and what I left, even to my appearance
but incidents will be no guide.
Time's wrong-way telescope will show
a minute man ten years hence
and by distance simplified.

Through that lens see if I seem
substance or nothing: of the world
deserving mention or charitable oblivion,

not by momentary spleen
or love into decision hurled,
leisurely arrive at an opinion.

Remember me when I am dead
and simplify me when I'm dead.

Keith Douglas

THE FURY OF AERIAL BOMBARDMENT

You would think the fury of aerial bombardment
Would rouse God to relent; the infinite spaces
Are still silent. He looks on shock-pried faces.
History, even, does not know what is meant.

You would feel that after so many centuries
God would give man to repent; yet he can kill
As Cain could, but with multitudinous will,
No farther advanced than in his ancient furies.

Was man made stupid to see his own stupidity?
Is God by definition indifference, beyond us all?
Is the eternal truth man's fighting soul
Wherein the Beast ravens in its own avidity?

Of Van Wettering I speak, and Averill,
Names on a list, whose faces I do not recall
But they are gone to early death, who late in school
Distinguished the belt feed lever from the belt holding pawl.

Richard Eberhart

MEMENTO

Remember the blackness of that flesh
Tarring the bones with a thin varnish
Belsen Theresenstadt Buchenwald where
Faces were a clenched despair
Knocking at the bird-song-fretted air.

Their eyes sunk jellied in their holes
Were held up to the sun like begging bowls
Their hands like rakes with finger-nails of rust
Scratched for a little kindness from the dust.
To many, in its beak, no dove brought answer.

Stephen Spender

HOMESICK

I've lived in the ghetto here more than a year,
In Terezin, in the black town now,
And when I remember my old home so dear,
I can love it more than I did, somehow.

Ah, home, home,
Why did they tear me away?
Here the weak die easy as a feather
And when they die, they die forever.

I'd like to go back home again,
It makes me think of sweet spring flowers.
Before, when I used to live at home,
It never seemed so dear and fair.

I remember now those golden days...
But maybe I'll be going there soon again.
People walk along the street,
You see at once on each you meet
That there's a ghetto here,
A place of evil and of fear.
There's little to eat and much to want,
Where bit by bit, it's horror to live.
But no one must give up!
The world turns and times change.

Yet we all hope the time will come
When we'll go home again.
Now I know how dear it is
And I often remember it.

Anonymous
(Written by a child in Theresenstadt
Concentration Camp, 1943.)

SECOND AUTUMN

So here am I
   Upon the German earth, beneath the German sky,
   And birds flock southward, wheeling as they fly,
   And there are morning mists, and trees turn brown,
   And the winds blow, and blow the dead leaves down
   And lamps are earlier on, and curtains drawn,
   And nights have frosted dew-drops on the lawn,
   And bonfire smoke goes crawling up on high,
Just as on English earth, beneath an English sky.
But here am I.

Patrick Savage

(POW 1941–45)

Part IV 1945 —
THE AGE OF ANXIETY

Background

The period since 1945 has been one of uneasy peace and frequent international crises—to use an already overtaxed phrase—an age of anxiety—with the constant threat of atomic war waiting ogre-like ready to pounce on the innocent defenceless prey of humanity. (At least the world would end not with a whimper, but a bang—and a big one at that!) The decades since 1945 have been times of recurrent crises—hatred and mutual distrust have split the wartime alliance of East and West, while racial and religious differences have split the nationhood of some of the great countries, and turned them into pits of turmoil and strife, hatred and despair. As in previous generations the poetry of the period reflects the atmosphere of its time.

'The Final Solution'

The Second World War, opening in September 1939 with the German attack on Poland, had as one of its final acts the liberation of a town named Oswiecim in Poland, the site of one of the greatest of extermination camps—Auschwitz. From early 1945 until the German surrender in May, it became more and more obvious that something pretty terrible had occurred in German-conquered countries. Gradually with the addition of names such as Belsen, Buchenwald, Ravensbruck, Theresenstadt, the extent of the horror of the extermination camps in which millions died became apparent. It seemed incomprehensible that the nation which could give the world a Bach and a Brahms, a Wagner and a Handel, a Freud and a Jung could also make such a degrading mark on the patchy record of the human race.

Some of the camps have been maintained as memorials and today people travel to see them just as in 1919 it was possible to tour the battlefields. The visitor finds a hill of human hair, a mound of cases and small personal possessions, the gas chambers, and incinerators. There is a great deal which is overpowering as a stimulus to the imagination and a challenge to the human conscience. Out of this what may be called a visitors' school of poetry has emerged—one which tries to express the feeling and emotion which comes with visiting such a place. Sylvia Plath wrote 'Daddy' after a visit to one camp, and Peter Porter's 'Annotations of Auschwitz' and 'Report to the Director' by George MacBeth were also written after visits to the death camps since 1945.

The Remembrance of War

The First World War has not yet lost its power over contemporary writers either. Each year Anzac Day and Remembrance Day offer a moment to think of the dead of both wars and to try to visualise what each war meant to those involved. Vernon Scannell's 'Remembrance Day' sees the subject critically but practically, without emotion;

> But wormy years have eaten their
> Identities and none can mourn
> These artificial dead.

On the other hand, Roger McGough illustrates another attitude to war—that it is in the past and to succeeding generations means less and less, as it slowly takes its place in history. 'On Picnics' is typical of this attitude. 'A Square Dance' takes a view of the Great War which would be unthinkable to Owen or Sassoon, or those involved in it—it could only come from those to whom the war is already history:

> In Flanders fields in Northern France
> They're all doing a brand new dance
> It makes you happy and out of breath
> And it's called the Dance of Death.
> Everybody stands in line
> Everybody's feeling fine
> We're all going to a hop
> 1–2–3 and over the top.
> It's the dance designed to thrill
> It's the mustard gas quadrille
> A dance for men—girls have no say in it
> For your partner is a bayonet.

See how the dancers sway and run
To the rhythm of the gun
Swing your partner dos-y-doed
All round the shells explode.
Honour your partner form a square
Smell the burning in the air
Over the barbed wire kicking high
Men like shirts hung out to dry.

If you fall that's no disgrace
Someone else can take your place
Old soldiers never die.........
......only young ones.

In Flanders fields where mortars blaze
They're all doing the latest craze
Khaki dancers out of breath
Doing the glorious Dance of Death
Doing the glorious (clap, clap) Dance of Death.

The Bomb

The explosion of the atomic bomb on Hiroshima and Nagasaki in August 1945 heralded the arrival of the atomic age, and before long the 'bomb' took its place as the subject of poetry, plays, novels, and general protest, best represented by the 'Ban the Bomb' movement of the 1950s. What happened in Hiroshima has been recorded by numerous poets and authors since that fateful day. John Hersey's 'Hiroshima' provides some interesting observations.

He [Dr Masakazu Fujii] saw the flash. To him—faced away from the centre and looking at his paper—it seemed a brilliant yellow. Startled, he began to rise to his feet. In that moment (he was 1,550 yards from the centre), the hospital leaned behind his rising and, with a terrible ripping noise, toppled into the river.

After the terrible flash—which, Father Kleinsorge later realised, reminded him of something he had read as a boy about a large meteor colliding with the earth—he had time (since he was 1,400 yards from the centre) for one thought! A bomb has fallen directly on us. Then, for a few seconds or minutes, he went out of his mind.

Naturally the people in Hiroshima did not have the faintest idea what an atomic bomb was. (Neither, for that matter, did many people outside Japan.)

At first, Dr Fujii could see only two fires, one across the river from his hospital site and one quite far to the south. But at the same time, he and his friend, [Dr Machii] observed something that puzzled them, and which, as doctors, they discussed: although there were as yet very few fires, wounded people were hurrying across the bridge in an endless parade of misery, and many of them exhibited terrible burns on their faces and arms. 'Why do you suppose it is?' Dr Fujii asked. Even a theory was comforting that day, and Dr Machii stuck to his. 'Perhaps because it was a Molotov Flower Basket,' he said.

A year after the explosion of the bomb,

Toshio Nakamura, who was ten at the time of the bombing, spoke freely, even gaily about the experience, and a few weeks before the anniversary wrote the following matter-of-fact essay for his teacher at No bori-cho Primary School:
The day before the bomb, I went for a swim. In the morning I was eating peanuts. I saw a light. I was knocked to my little sister's sleeping place. When we were saved I could only see as far as the tram. My mother and I started to pack our things. The neighbours were walking around burned and bleeding. Hataya-san told me to run away with her. I said I wanted to wait for my mother. We went to the park. A whirlwind came. At night a gas tank burned and I saw the reflection in the river. We stayed in the park one night. Next day I went to Taiko Bridge and met my friends Kikuki and Murakemi. They were looking for their mothers. But Kikuki's mother was wounded and Murakami's mother, alas, was dead.

The logical development of the V1 and V2 rockets of the war, are the ICBMs etc. equipped with atomic warheads which exist today. The 1950s saw the construction of the DEW line (Distant Early Warning) in Canada, the establishment of the Strategic Air Command, and practically annual international crises. This in turn gave rise to a series of poems of which 'Missile Commander' by George MacBeth is representative. The fear of accidental war increased in proportion to the improvements in rocketry and the sophistication of weapons, while the poets continued to express the doubts they have about these further refinements.

Vietnam

The most recent war to concern poets has been the conflict in Vietnam—one which has created concern among people around the world. There is strong feeling both for and against Vietnam, but few on either side seem fully informed on whatever view they choose to support. At the moment it is difficult to judge just what value this poetry will have. Like most poetry of any war period, it is emotional, meant to attract attention, or glorify one aspect or another—a tale of sound, fury and sometimes tears, more often than not meaning very little, if anything at all. Adrian Mitchell's 'Norman Morrison' deals with an occurrence in 1965. 'To Whom It May Concern' tries to convey its meaning and effect by means of repetition—a most effective technique. James K. Baxter, whose father suffered greatly for his views on warfare, holds strong views not only on Vietnam, but war generally. His poetry denounces warfare—'The Ballad of Grady's Dream' exploits a situation confronting New Zealand troops in the Middle East, and goes some way to destroying the 'god on our side' myth, which Bob Dylan wrote of in his song. 'A Takapuna Business Man Considers his Son's Death in Korea' tells of the loss felt by parents who lose a child in war. Among his Vietnam poems 'Song of the Dying Gunner' is perhaps the most commendable.

Holding the Flag

The love of one's country is something which most people share in common, and many have died to uphold this love. Unfortunately, it has often been abused. Conscientious objection was, and still is, seen by many people as both cowardly and unpatriotic, while some people can go to the opposite direction and become over patriotic and bigoted. It was a Serbian patriot, Gustav Princip, who fired the shot that sparked the First World War. Today patriotism is still something that is necessary for a country to survive, but in many quarters there seems to be a wider understanding of what is patriotic and what is not. Many songs and poems have been written on the subject of patriotism. In 1957 the Irish playwright Dominic Behan wrote 'The Patriot Game' after the death of an IRA member, Fergal O'Hanlon, and an Irish poet, Sean South, in an IRA attack on Dungarren Barracks.

> Come all you young rebels,
> And list while I sing.
> For love of one's land
> Is a terrible thing.
> It banishes fear
> Like the speed of a flame
> And makes us all part of
> The patriot game.

In opposition to Behan is Roger McGough, whose 'Why Patriots are a Bit Nuts in the Head' needs no comment:

> Patriots are a bit nuts in the head
> because they wear
> red, white and blue—
> tinted spectacles
> (red for blood
> white for glory
> and blue...
> for a boy.)
> And are in effervescent danger
> of losing their lives
> lives are good for you
> when you are alive
> You can eat and drink a lot
> and go out with girls
> (sometimes if you are lucky
> you can even go to bed with them)
> but you can't do this
> if you have your belly shot away
> and your seeds
> spread over some corner of a foreign field
> to facilitate
> in later years
> the growing of oats by some peasant yobbo.
>
> When you are posthumous it is cold and dark
> and that is why patriots are a bit nuts in the head.

This is perhaps rather typical of the trend in modern literature—to revalue the old mores which older generations have upheld. In the theatre, music, art, motion picture, nothing is any longer sacrosanct, no value too revered, and in the field of war literature this is especially true. McGough's 'On Picnics' is an example of this new impetus. Other modern authors have parodied what has come before. *Punch* recently had this poem—a parody of Brooke's 'The Soldier'.

The poem refers to the Arabs in Egypt during and after the Second World War, to whom the British Army supply bases were indeed a gift from Allah, not to be bypassed.

> If I should drool, think only this of me:
>   That there's some corned beef in that left hand field
> That has been Made in England. There must be
>   In those fat sacks a fatter prize concealed;
> Dried egg that England bore, shaped, put in tins,
>   And Crosse and Blackwell's full-fruit damson jam,
> Brazil's pork pies, forced meat in sausage skins,
>   Heinz pea soup, Peek Frean biscuits, Yorkshire ham.
> And think! Tinned heart, all offal cut away!
>   Pilchards eternal, kept in brine, no less!
>   A flavour all their own, by England given;
> Her bully beef, her tea, fresh as the day
>   She packed them. Cans of such choice tenderness:
> Braised hearts and peas, done in an English oven.

Examples of this attitude change appear in literature also. The most notable example to date is Joseph Heller's *Catch–22* in which an American air force officer, Colonel Cathcart, keeps raising the number of missions his men must fly before returning home, so that the Pentagon will speed up his promotion.

Like all the other officers at Group Headquarters except Major Darby, Colonel Cathcart was infused with the democratic spirit: he believed that all his men were created equal, and he therefore spurned all men outside Group Headquarters with equal fervour. Nevertheless, he believed in his men. As he told them frequently in the briefing room, he believed they were at least ten missions better than any other outfit and felt that any who did not share this confidence he had placed in them could get the hell out. The only way they could get the hell out, though, as Yossarian learned when he flew to visit ex-P.F.C. Wintergreen, was by flying the extra ten missions.

Inevitably most of the men become hopeless psychotics, through sheer exasperation:

'Is Orr crazy?'

'He sure is,' Doc Danecka said.

'Can you ground him?'

'I sure can. But first he has to ask me. That's part of the rule.'

'Then why doesn't he ask you to?'

'Because he's crazy,' Doc Danecka said. 'He has to be crazy to keep flying combat missions after all the close calls he's had. Sure, I can ground Orr. But first he has to ask me to.'

'That's all he has to do to be grounded?'

'That's all. Let him ask me.'

'And then you can ground him?' Yossarian asked

'No. Then I can't ground him.'

'You mean there's a catch?'

'Sure there's a catch,' Doc Danecka replied. 'Catch–22. Anyone who wants to get out of combat duty isn't really crazy.'

There was only one catch, and that was Catch–22, which specified that a concern for one's own safety in the face of dangers that were real and immediate was the process of a rational mind. Orr was crazy and could be grounded. All he had to do was ask; and as soon as he did, he would no longer be crazy and would have to fly more missions. Orr would be crazy to fly more missions and sane if he didn't, but if he was sane he had to fly them. If he flew them he was crazy and didn't have to; but if he didn't want to he was sane and had to. Yossarian was moved very deeply by the absolute simplicity of this clause of Catch–22 and let out a respectful whistle.

'That's some catch, that Catch–22,' he observed.

'It's the best there is,' Doc Danecka agreed.

The combination of the comic and the tragic portrayed in *Catch–22* is found in another novel, recently a motion picture *M.A.S.H.* (Mobile Army Surgical Hospital), which comments on the military medical system in the Korean War.

While attitudes have been satirically anti-war, at times, strong feelings about the injustice and futility of it all have been expressed by many. Bob Dylan the poet/folk singer of the 1960s–70s affected the self-righteous attitude of many people in 'With God on Our Side'.

'Universal Soldier' was written by the American Indian folk singer, Buffy St Marie, in Toronto in 1963, at the time of the debates as to whether or not Canada should accept nuclear warheads from the United States. It has, however, a wider meaning and illustrates a theme which has been more and more popular in the last twenty years—the concept of the Universal Soldier—standing for no particular nation or ideology, but embracing one and all.

He's five foot two and he's six feet four.
He fights with missiles and with spears,
He's all of thirty-one and he's only seventeen.
He's been a soldier for a thousand years.
He's a Catholic, a Hindu, an athiest, a Jain,
A Buddist and a Baptist and a Jew,
And he knows he shouldn't kill
and he knows he always will,
Kill you for me, my friend,
And me for you.
And he's fighting for Canada,
He's fighting for France,
He's fighting for the U.S.A.
And he's fighting for the Russians
And he's fighting for Japan,
And he thinks we'll put an end to war that way.
And he's fighting for democracy,
He's fighting for the Reds,
He says it's for the peace of all.
He's the one who must decide
Who's to live and who's to die,
And he never sees the writing on the wall.

But without him how could Hitler
Have condemned him at Dachau,
Without him Caesar would have stood alone,
He's the one who gives his body
As a weapon of the war,
And without him all this killing can't go on.
He's the Universal Soldier
And he really is to blame,
His orders come from far away no more,
They come from him and you and me,
And brothers, can't you see
This is not the way we put an end to war.

This concept is perhaps best summed up by Yevgeny Yevtushenko in *A Precocious Autobiography* in his description of a visit to Moscow in the days when the German Army was knocking on the very gates of the city.

In '41 Mama took me back to Moscow. There I saw our enemies for the first time. If my memory is right, nearly twenty thousand German war prisoners were to be marched in a single column through the streets of Moscow.

The pavements swarmed with onlookers, cordoned off by soldiers and police.

The crowd were mostly women—Russian women with hands roughened by hard work, lips untouched by lipstick and thin hunched shoulders which had borne half the burden of the war. Every one of them must have had a father or a husband, a brother or a son killed by the Germans.

They gazed with hatred in the direction from which the column was to appear.

At last we saw it.

The generals marched at the head, massive chins stuck out, lips folded disdainfully, their whole demeanour meant to show superiority over their plebeian victors.

'They smell of eau-de-cologne, the bastards', someone in the crowd said with hatred.

The women were clenching their fists. The soldiers and policemen had all they could do to hold them back.

All at once something happened to them.

They saw German soldiers, thin, unshaven, wearing dirty blood-stained bandages, hobbling on crutches or leaning on the shoulders of their comrades; the soldiers walked with their heads down.

The street became dead silent—the only sound was the shuffling of boots and the thumping of crutches.

Then I saw an elderly woman in broken-down boots push herself forward and touch a policeman's shoulder saying: 'Let me through'. There must have been something about her that made him step aside.

She went up to the column, took from inside her coat something wrapped in a coloured handkerchief and unfolded it. It was a crust of black bread. She pushed it awkwardly into the pocket of a soldier, so exhausted that he was tottering on his feet. And now suddenly from every side women were running towards the soldiers, pushing into their hands bread, cigarettes, whatever they had.

The soldiers were no longer enemies.

They were people.

From **RECAPITULATIONS (13)**

When nuns were spitted and poets fell
And Spain the medieval hell
Became our modern one as well
    And I, a Hamlet, held my tongue
    Tell me, conscience, was I wrong?

When matters on the Ebro failed
And Cornford died and Campbell railed
And I to my Tahiti sailed
    To ape Loti and Rupert's throng
    Tell me, conscience, was I wrong?

When Russia smote the sledded Finn
And generals of the French let in
Germans to practice mutual sin,
    And I read Horace all night long,
    Tell me, conscience, was I wrong?

When London like a phoenix burned
And flew in fire and fire returned
And peace beneath and the umbrella spurned,
    Did I to either side belong,
    Tell me, conscience, was I wrong?

When dolls in armour from their toys
Scuttled our fleet with frightful noise
And I obeyed the White House voice,
    My best friend was in prison flung.
    Tell me, conscience, was I wrong?

Karl Shapiro

RETURNED SOLDIER

The boy who volunteered at seventeen
At twenty-three is heavy on the booze.
Strafed in the desert and bombed out in Crete—
With sore dark eyes and hardened by the heat
Entitled now to call himself a man
And in the doll's-house walk with death-at-ease;
The Cairo women, cobbers under sand
A death too great for dolls to understand.

Back to a city bed or station hut
At maelstrom centre falling through the night
To dreams where deeper than El Alamein
A buried childhood stirs with leaves and flowers
Remembered girls, the blurred and bitter waters.
Wakes to the midnight rafters and the rain.

James K. Baxter

From **RECAPITULATIONS (2)**

At one the Apocalypse had spoken,
Von Moltke fell, I was housebroken.

At two how could I understand
The murder of Archduke Ferdinand?

France was involved with history,
I with my thumbs when I was three.

A sister came, we neared a war,
Paris was shelled when I was four.

I joined in our peach-kernel drive
For poison gas when I was five.

At six I cheered the big parade,
Burned sparklers and drank lemonade.

At seven I passed at school though I
Was far too young to say Versailles.

At eight the boom began to tire,
I tried to set our house on fire.

The Bolshevists had drawn the line,
Lenin was striken, I was nine.

What evils do not retrograde
To my first odious decade?

Karl Shapiro

THANKSGIVING (1956)

a monstering horror swallows
this unworld me by you
as the god of our fathers' fathers bows
to a which that walks like a who

but the voice-with-a-smile of democracy
announces night & day
"all poor little peoples that want to be free
just trust in the u s a"

suddenly uprose hungary
and she gave a terrible cry
"no slave's unlife shall murder me
for i will freely die"

she cried so high thermopylae
heard her and maraton
and all prehuman history
and finally The UN

"be quiet little hungary
and do as you are bid
a good kind bear is angary
we fear for the quo pro quid"

uncle sam shrugs his pretty
pink shoulders you know how
and he twitches a liberal titty
and lisps "i'm busy right now"

so rah-rah-rah democracy
let's all be thankful as hell
and bury the statue of liberty
(because it begins to smell)

E.E. Cummings

JEWS AT HAIFA

The freighter, gray with rust,
Coasts to a bare wharf of the harbour.
From the funnel's shade (the arbour
Of gourds from which the prophet, without trust,
Watched his old enemies,
The beings of the earth) I scrutinize

The hundreds at the rail
Lapped in the blue blaze of this sea
Who stare till their looks fail
At the earth that they are promised; silently
See the sandbagged machine-guns,
The red-kneed soldiers blinking in the sun.

A machine-gun away
Are men with our faces: we are torn
With the live blaze of day—
Till we feel shifting, wrenched apart, the worn
Name stones of our last knowledge:
That all men wish our death. Here on the edge

Of the graves of Europe
We believe: truly, we are not dead;
It seems to us that hope
Is possible—that even mercy is permitted
To men on this earth,
To Jews on this earth . . . But at Cyprus, the red earth,

The huts, the trembling wire
That wreathes us, are to us familiar
As death. All night, the fires
Float their sparks up to the yellow stars;
From the steel, stilted tower
The light sweeps over us. We whisper: 'Ours.'

Ours, and the stones slide home.
There is no hope; 'in all this world
There is no other wisdom
Than ours: we have understood the world,'
We think; but hope, in dread
Search for one doubt, and whisper: 'Truly we are not dead.'

Randall Jarrell

THE MONUMENTS OF HIROSHIMA

The roughly estimated ones, who do not sort well with our common
    phrases.
Who are by no means eating roots dandelion, or pushing up the
    daisies

The more or less anonymous, to whom no human idiom can apply
Who neither passed away, or on,
    nor went before, nor vanished on a sigh.

Little of peace for them to rest in, less of them to rest in peace:
Dust to dust a swift transition, ashes to ashes with awful ease.
Their only monument will be of others' casting—
A Tower of Peace, a Hall of Peace, a Bridge of Peace
    —who might have wished for something lasting,
Like a wooden box.

D.J. Enright

VICTORY MARCH

WHAT DID YOU BUILD THE TROPHY OF, SOLDIER, SOLDIER?
Of bottles, broken parasols and bones in blackened tanks
Of mud and mines and message-pads, of shells and charabancs
    Of chamber-pots and panzerfaust, of jerricans and jeeps
    Of carrion and cratered roads, of rust and rubbish-heaps.

WHAT WAS YOUR MARCHING MUSIC, SOLDIER, SOLDIER?
The sons of morning singing the glory of the Word
Set thunder clouds a-ringing, but all we heard
    Was the tunes of Tinpan Alley from a million radios
    And the wind lamenting where the river flows.

WHAT WILL BE YOUR DREAM TONIGHT, SOLDIER, SOLDIER?
I shall see children playing in the rubble of a street
And a girl who turned to folly for a tin of meat
    I shall hear an old man weeping by a broken door
    And I shan't sleep so easy as the lads who march no more.

M.K. Joseph

SALAD DAYS 1914

The flags that were
furling fell from the
half mast and started
patting one another in
the bushes
quite softly to begin with.

Spike Hawkins.

HAIFA BAY IN THE MORNING

I saw a ship come sailing in,
Sailing in, sailing in,
With a list like a stormtrooper's twisted grin
At Haifa Bay in the morning.

The Army boat was waiting there,
(Haganah flashed 'Take care! Take care!')
The amiable squaddies all a'stare
Just three miles out in the morning.

And I was there in my little press boat
With one stout Guardsman to keep it afloat
And a man from The Times who claimed he wrote
And a blasé photographer yawning.

Their lousy ship they bought from a Greek,
That it ever arrived was a flaming freak
Considering the size of its list and leak
Off Palestine in the morning.

Through shortage of water two girls had died
(Gone to their dreams of a Sabra's bride),
But two young boys jumped over the side
As the troopship moved close in the morning.

They could see the coast of the Holy Land
And the beckoning gleam of Haifa's sand
And hoped for Haganah to give them a hand
To lose themselves in the morning.

But I was there with my little press launch
Full of zeal with my Guardsman staunch,
And when the two Zionists ceased to float
We hauled them up in our little press boat
And tried to explain they'd come to no harm.

(Both had numbers tattooed on their arms
In a quaint old Belsen warning.)

My Guardsman, a reprobate Irish Mick,
Albeit a lapsed Catholick,
Said 'Give the poor devils a chance to run
And then we'll go back and face the fun'.
His Paddy's face white in the morning.

But the immigrant ship was towed to the quay
And the two little Zionists brought in by me;
One old Jew jumped over the side
And kissed the ground and cried and cried;
Another leapt down and split his head
And bled an Hebraic script of red
On the Holy Quay in the morning.

An Army troopship took them away
With swift discretion the very next day
And Haifa wept as they sailed away
To a Cyprus camp in the morning.

ENVOI

They all are back in Israel now
And the two young Zionists work at the plough,
And my stalwart drunken Irish Mick
Is a reformed much-married Catholick.
But my mind it goes back to Haifa Bay,
And dwells on the words I dared not say
And the sorrowful ship that sailed away
From the Holy Land in the morning.

Michael Ivens

SONNET TO MACARTHUR'S EYES

General MacArthur looked down on the bodies of four young Korean
soldiers. 'That's a good sight for my old eyes', he said.

Newspaper Report

I have known old eyes that have seen many more
    aspects of warfare than this man has seen—
    eyes that had looked on Gallipoli or the keen
    edge of battle with the Boers or even in colder war
    had known Balaclava and the Mutiny's evil score:
    such eyes as I've known them old have always been
    eager to see spring flowers and the youth who mean
    mankind's spring after war's winter. Never before

Have I known of anyone whose old eyes rejoice
    to see young men lying dead in their own land,
    never have I known one who of his own choice
    follows up the machines of death to take his stand
    over the slain and in a quivering voice
    disclaim his joy at youth dead before his hand.

R.A.K. Mason
(September 1950)

TWENTIETH-CENTURY MOTHER

Rocking the cradle of his child
I used to watch the bombers wane,
And wish him peace and wish them well.
For then my heart was reconciled
To bombs, theirs, ours, the heartless rain
On just, unjust. O what the hell!
To stop the killing sooner, I,
We all, must think of ends, not means...
(And that became my rock-a-bye)
There could be peace before she weans.

Our child now marches through the town,
Bearing her own child as she goes,
To point the slogan, to protest
Against a threat that no one knows
From faceless men of no renown.
No what-the-hell: no for-the-best.
There are no ends: spare us the means.
There could be war before she weans.

John Pudney
(1967)

From **ELEGY FOR AN UNKNOWN SOLDIER**

There was a time when I would magnify
His ending; scatter words as if I wept
Tears not of my own but man's; there was a time.
But not now so. He died of a common sickness.

Awkward at school, he could not master sums.
Could you expect him then to understand
The miracle and menace of his body
That grew as mushrooms grow from dusk to dawn?

He had the weight, though, for a football scrum,
And thought it fine to listen to the cheering
And drink beer with the boys, telling them tall
Stories of girls he had never known.

But when the War came he was glad and sorry,
But soon enlisted. Then his mother cried
A little, and his father boasted how
He'd let him go, though needed for the farm.

Likely in Egypt he would find out something
About himself, if flies and drunkeness
And deadly heat could tell him much—until
In his first battle a shell splinter caught him.

So crown him with memorial bronze among
The older dead, child of a mountainous island.

Who born of silence has burned back to silence.

James K. Baxter

PIG ISLAND LETTERS (8)

When I was only semen in a gland
Or less than that, my father hung
From a torture post at Mud Farm
Because he would not kill. The guards
Fried sausages, and as the snow came darkly
I feared a death by cold in the groin
And plotted revolution. His black and swollen thumbs
Explained the brotherhood of man,

But he is old now in his apple garden
And we have seen our strong Antaeus die
In the glass castle of the bureaucracies
Robbing our bread of salt. Shall Marx and Christ
Share beds this side of Jordan? I set now
Unwillingly these words down:
'Political action in its source is pure,
Human, direct, but in its civil function
Becomes the jail it laboured to destroy'.

James K. Baxter

. . . .

o to be in finland
now that russia's here

swing low
sweet ca

rr
y on

pass the freedoms pappy or
uncle shylock not interested

E.E. Cummings

SONG TO FIDEL

You said the sun would rise.
Let's go
along those unmapped paths
to free the green alligator you love.

And let's go obliterating
insults with our
brows swept with dark insurgent stars.
We shall have victory or shoot past death.

At the first shot the whole jungle
will awake with fresh amazement and
there and then serene company
we'll be at your side.

When your voice quarters the four winds
reforma agraria, justice, bread, freedom,
we'll be there with identical accents
at your side.

And when the clean operation against the tyrant
ends at the end of the day
there and then set for the final battle
we'll be at your side.

And when the wild beast licks his wounded side
where the dart of Cuba hits him
we'll be at your side
with proud hearts.

Don't ever think our integrity can be sapped
by those decorated fleas hopping with gifts
we want their rifles, their bullets and a rock
nothing else.

And if iron stands in our way
we ask for a sheet of Cuban tears
to cover our guerrilla bones
on the journey to American history.
Nothing more.

Ernesto Che Guevara

The spirit of renewal, the desire that we should excel collectively,
an awareness of a higher destiny: all this we feel incomparably more
deeply. We had heard so often of those things and had assumed that
the abstract words that described them referred to something
beautiful; but now we are living that beauty, feeling it with all our
senses and it is truly unique. The way our small world here in the
Sierra has developed is unbelievable. The phrase 'the people', which
so often has a vague and confused meaning, has here been
transformed into something marvellously and immediately real. Now
I really know who 'the people' are: I recognise them in this
invisible strength which protects us on all sides.

(*Fidel Castro*, in a letter to Frank Pais,
Sierra Maestra, 21 July 1957.)

A DEAD YOUTH

A dead youth. How can he turn the heart of a rifle,
How inflict the shades of nothingness with suffering.
But through his wounds a thing from our lives
escapes, gone over the hill forever.

The large isolation of the hero is his martyrdom.
Don't walk away from him.

Fernando Gordillo Cervantes

THE PRICE OF A COUNTRY

3,000,000 is the pricemark on a country
if somebody wants to sell it
and someone wanted to
                        and did.
Later they said
            his sons
were born just to sing it.

Just as if battle is not the most unmistakeable
of songs
or death the most grand.

'About the events (and the attitudes which made these events
possible) which led to the conclusion or the Bryan-Chamorro treaty
between Nicaragua and the U.S.A. in 1916.'

Fernando Gordillo Cervantes

POEM

No,
I don't
laugh
at death.
It's just
that I'm
not afraid to die
among
birds
and trees

Javier Heraud

HAVANA 1959

Out of so much talking
the chains lost their voices
night was subjected
to dawn
death took away
its forked tail
plague fled
with his black sabre on his shoulder
clocks became
eyeless
without shores of skin
without black boots
hunger wandered out
leaving behind its thousand witnessess
the owner of the vine lost his
pants
and the master lost his shadow.

Marco Antonio Flores

SNIPERS

When I was kneehigh to a tabletop,
Uncle Tom came home from Burma.
He was the youngest of seven brothers
so the street borrowed extra bunting
and whitewashed him a welcome.

All the relations made the pilgrimage,
including us, laughed, sang, made a fuss.
He was brown as a chairleg,
drank tea out of a white mug the size of my head
and said next to nowt.

But every few minutes he would scan
the ceiling nervously hands begin to shake.
'For snipers', everyone later agreed,
'A difficult habit to break'.

Sometimes when the two of us were alone,
he'd have a snooze after dinner
and I'd keep an eye open for Japs.
Of course, he didn't know this
and the tanner he'd give me before I went
was for keeping quiet,
but I liked to think it was money well spent.

Being Uncle Tom's secret bodyguard
Had it's advantages, the pay was good
and the hours were short, but even so,
the novelty soon wore off, and instead,
I started school and became an infant.

Later, I learnt that he was in a mental home.
'Needn't tell anybody...Nothing serious
...Delayed shock...Usual sort of thing
...Completely cured now the doctors say'.
The snipers came down from the ceiling
but they didn't go away.

Over the next five years they picked off
three of his brothers; one of whom was my father.
No glory, no citations,
Bang! straight through the heart.

Uncle Tom's married now, with a family.
He doesn't say much, but each night after tea,
he still dozes fitfully in his favourite armchair.
(dreams by courtesy of Henri Rousseau).
He keeps out of the sun, and listens now and then
for the tramp tramp of the Colonel Bogeymen.
He knows damn well he's still at war,
just that the snipers aren't Japs anymore.

Roger McGough

ON PICNICS

at the goingdown of the sun
and in the morning
i try to remember them
but their names are ordinary names
and their causes are thighbones
tugged excitedly from the soil
by frenchchildren
on picnics

Roger McGough

MOTHER THE WARDROBE IS FULL OF INFANTRYMEN

mother the wardrobe is full of infantrymen
i did i asked them
but they snarled saying it was a mans life

mother there is a centurion tank in the parlour
i did i asked the officer
but he laughed saying 'Queens regulations'
(piano was out of tune anyway)

mother polish your identity bracelet
there is a mushroom cloud in the backgarden
i did i tried to bring in the cat
but it simply came to pieces in my hand
i did i tried to white-wash the windows
but there weren't any
i did i tried to hide under the stairs
but i couldn't get in for civil defence leaders
i did i tried to ring candid camera
but they crossed their hearts

i went for a policeman but they were looting the town
i went for a fire engine but they were all upside down
i went for a priest but they were all on their knees
mother don't just lie there say something please
mother don't just lie there say something please

Roger McGough

LANCE-CORPORAL DIXON

I saw a picture in the paper the other day
Of a soldier carrying a baby.
Lance-corporal Dixon was his name.
The baby?
His C.O.'s daughter.
My mother was touched by the picture,
Said it was charming
That a man so tough
Could be so gentle.
It looked odd to me:
A sten gun under one arm,
A baby under the other.

Linda Newton

THE ENLISTED MAN

Yelled, Corporal Punishment at Private Reasons:
  'Rebels like you have no right to enlist—
    or to exist!'
Major Considerations leered approval,
  Clenching his fist,
    And gave his fierce moustache a fiercer twist.
So no appeal, even to General Conscience,
  Kept Private Reasons off the defaulter-list.

Robert Graves

WEDDING

Those weddings in wartime! The deceiving comfort!
The dishonesty of words about living.
Sonorous snowy roads.
In the wind's wicked teeth I hurry down them
to a hasty wedding at the next village.
With worn-out tread and hair down in my eyes
I go inside, I famous for my dancing,
into the noisy house.
In there tensed up with nerves and with emotion
among a crowd of friends and family,
called up, distraught, the bridegroom
sitting beside his Vera, his bride.
Will in a few days put his greatcoat on
and set out coated for the war.
Will see new country, carry a rifle.
May also drop if he is hit.
His glass is fizzing but he can't drink it.
The first night may be the last night.
And sadly eyeing me and bitter-minded
he leans in his despair across the table
and says, 'Come on then, dance.'
Drinks are forgotten. Everyone looks round.
Out I twirl to begin. Clap of my feet.
Shake.
      Scrape the floor with my toe-cap.
Whistle. Whistle. Slap hands.
Faster, leaping ceiling-high.
Moving the posters pinned on the walls:
HITLER KAPUT
           Her eyes streaming with tears.
Already soaked in sweat and out of breath—
'Dance.'
They cry out in despair, and I dance.

When I get home my feet are log-heavy:
some drunken people from another wedding
turn up behind me. Mother must let me go.
The scene again: I see it, and again
beside the edge of a trailing tablecloth
I squat down to dance.
          She weeping
and her friends weeping. I frightened
don't feel like dancing, but you can't not dance.

Yevgeny Yevtushenko

LATER

Oh what a sobering,
what a talking-to from conscience afterwards:
the short moment of frankness at the party
and the enemy crept up.
But to have learnt nothing is terrible,
and peering earnest eyes are terrible
detecting secret thoughts is terrible
in simple words and immature disturbance.
This diligent suspicion has no merit.
The blinded judges are no public servants.
It would be far more terrible to mistake
a friend than to mistake an enemy.

Yevgeny Yevtushenko

GREAT WAR POEMS

1 The same old soldiers walking along the same old skyline

2 Dead hand through the sandbags reaching out for the cream-and-white butterfly

3 mud/water under duckboards/mud/rats scamper in starshell darkness/mud/smell of shit and rotting bodies/mud/resting your sweaty forehead on the sandbags OVER THE TOP the first men in the lunar landscape.

4 'What did you do to the Great Whore, Daddy?'

5 Poppies slightly out-of-focus and farmcarts bringing in the peaceful dead.

6 The ghost of Wilfred Owen selling matches outside the Burlington Arcade.

7 Seafog. Red flaring lights from the shorebatteries. The roar of shells rattle of machineguns. Water running in the bilges. My feet slipping on the damp cobbles of the quayside.

8 DON'T BE VAGUE—BLAME GENERAL HAIG.

9 four white feathers clutched in a bloodstained envelope.

10 a skull nestling in a bed of wild strawberries/boots mouldering green with fungus/saplings thrusting through rusting helmets/ sunken barges drifting full of leaves down autumn rivers.

Adrian Henri

SLEEP NOW

Sleep now,
Your blood moving in the quiet wind;
No longer afraid of the rabbits
Hurrying through the tall grass
Or the faces laughing on the beach
And among the cold trees.

Sleep now,
Alone in the sleeves of grief,
Listening to the clothes falling
And to your flesh touching God;
To the chatter and backslapping
Of Christ meeting heroes of war.

Sleep now,
Your words have passed
The lights shining from the East
And the sound of the flack
Raping graves and emptying seasons.

You do not hear the dry wind pray
Or the children play
A game called 'Soldiers' in the street.

Brian Patten

AFTER A WAR

The outcome? Conflicting rumours
As to what faction murdered
The one man who, had he survived,
Might have ruled us without corruption.
Not that it matters now:
We're busy collecting the dead,
Counting them, hard though it is.
To be sure what side they were on.
What's left of their bodies and faces
Tells of no need but for burial,
The mutilation was practised
By Right, Left and Centre alike.
As for the children and women
Who knows what they wanted
Apart from the usual things?
Food is scarce now, and men are scarce,
Whole villages burnt to the ground,
New cities in disrepair.

The war is over. Somebody must have won.
Somebody will have won, when peace is declared.

Michael Hamburger

FIFTEEN MILLION PLASTIC BAGS

I was walking in a government warehouse
Where the daylight never goes.
I saw fifteen million plastic bags
Hanging in a thousand rows.

Five million bags were six feet long
Five million bags were five foot five
Five million were stamped with Mickey Mouse
And they came in a smaller size.

Were they for guns or uniforms
Or a dirty kind of party game?
Then I saw each bag had a number
And every bag bore a name.

And five million bags were six feet long
Five million were five foot five
Five million were stamped with Mickey Mouse
And they came in a smaller size.

So I've taken my bag from the hanger
And I've pulled it over my head
And I'll wait for the priest to zip it
So the radiation won't spread.

Now five million bags are six feet long
Five million are five foot five
Five million are stamped with Mickey Mouse
And they come in a smaller size.

Adrian Mitchell

ORDER ME A TRANSPARENT COFFIN AND DIG MY CRAZY GRAVE

After the next war . . . and the sky
Heaves with contaminated rain.
End to end our bodies lie
Round the world and back again.

Now from their concrete suites below
Statesmen demurely emanate,
And down the lines of millions go
To see the people lie in state.

Nikita Ikes, Franco de Gaulles,
Officiate and dig the holes.
Mao tse-Sheks, Macadenauers,
Toting artificial flowers.

As they pay tribute each one wishes
The rain was less like tears, less hot, less thick.
They mutter, wise as blind white fishes,
Occasionally they are sick.

But I drily grin from my perspex coffin
As they trudge till they melt into the wet,
And I say: 'Keep on walking, keep on walking,
You bastards, you've got a hell of a way to walk yet.'

Adrian Mitchell

PEACH, PLUM, OR APRICOT

Peach, Plum, or Apricot!
How much money have you got?
If you've got a bob or two,
I will bring some home for you.

Apricot, Peach, or Plum!
We may get blown to kingdom come,
Let us eat our fruit before
Our parents go again to war.

Plum, Apricot, or Peach!
Hide the stone from out their reach,
So that it falls into the earth
And brings another world to birth.

Bernard Kops

THIS EXCELLENT MACHINE

This excellent machine is neatly planned,
A child, a half-wit would not feel perplexed:
No chance to err, you simply press the button—
At once each cog in motion moves the next,
The whole revolves, and everything that lives
Is quickly sucked towards the running band,
Where, shot between the automatic knives,
It's guaranteed to finish dead as mutton.

This excellent machine will illustrate
The modern world divided into nations:
So neatly planned, that if you merely tap it
The armaments will start their devastations,
And though we're for it, though we're all convinced
Some fool will press the button soon or late,
We stand and stare, expecting to be minced,—
And very few are asking 'Why not scrap it?'

John Lehmann

TELLING LIES TO THE YOUNG IS WRONG

Telling lies to the young is wrong.
Proving to them that lies are true is wrong.
Telling them God's in his heaven
and all's well with the world is wrong.
The young know what you mean. The young are people.
Tell them the difficulties can't be counted,
and let them see not only what will be
but see with clarity these present times.
Say obstacles exist they must encounter
sorrow happens, hardship happens.
The hell with it. Who never knew
the price of happiness will not be happy.
Forgive no error you recognise,
it will repeat itself, increase,
and afterwards our pupils
will not forgive in us what we forgave.

Yevgeny Yevtushenko

THE RESPONSIBILITY

I am the man who gives the word,
If it should come, to use the Bomb.
I am the man who spreads the word
From him to them if it should come.

I am the man who gets the word
From him who spreads the word from him.

I am the man who drops the Bomb
If ordered by one who's heard
From him who merely spreads the word
The first one gives it if it should come.

I am the man who loads the Bomb
That he must drop should orders come
From him who gets the word passed on
By one who waits to hear from him.

I am the man who makes the Bomb
That he must load for him to drop
If told by one who gets the word
From one who passes it from him.

I am the man who fills the till,
Who pays the tax, who foots the bill
That guarantees the Bomb he makes
For him to load for him to drop
If orders come from one who gets
The word passed on to him by one
Who waits to hear it from the man
Who gives the word to use the Bomb.

I am the man behind it all;
I am the one responsible.

Peter Appleton

PARABLE

Two neighbours, who were rather dense,
Considered that their mutual fence
Were more symbolic of their peace
(Which they maintained would never cease)
If each about his house and garden
Set up a more substantial warden.
Quickly they cleared away the fence
To build a wall at great expense;
And soon their little plots of ground
Were barricaded all around:
Yet still they added stone to stone,
As if they never would be done,
For when one neighbour seemed to tire
The other shouted: Higher! Higher!
Thus day by day in their unease,
They built the battlements of peace
Whose shadows, like a gathering plot,
Until the ground, so overcast,
Became a rank and weedy waste.

Now in obsession, they uprear;
Jealous, and proud, and full of fear:
And, lest they halt for lack of stone,
They pull their dwelling-houses down.
At last, by their insane excess,
Their ramparts guard a wilderness;
And hate, arousing out of shame,
Flares up into a wonderous flame:
They curse; they strike; they break the wall
Which buries them beneath its fall.

William Soutar

LITTLE JOHNNY'S CONFESSION

This morning
   being rather young and foolish
   I borrowed a machine gun my father
   had left hidden since the war, went out,
   and eliminated a number of small enemies.
   Since then I have not returned home.

This morning
   swarms of police with trackerdogs
   wander about the city
   with my description printed
   on their minds, asking:
   'Have you seen him?
   He is seven years old,
   likes Pluto, Mighty Mouse
   and Biffo the Bear,
   have you see him, anywhere?

This morning
   sitting alone in a strange playground
   muttering you've blundered, you've blundered
   over and over to myself
   I work out my next move
   but cannot move.
   The trackerdogs will sniff me out,
   they have my lollypops.

Brian Patten

LITTLE JOHNNY'S FOOLISH INVENTION

A Fable for Atomic Adam

One day
   while playing with old junk in the attic
   Little Johnny accidentally invented an atomic bomb
   and not knowing what to do with it
   buried it in the front garden.

Next morning
   during cornflakes and sunrise
   he noticed it glowing damp among the cabbages
   and so took it out
   out into the city
   where it smelt of tulips
   but was sadly inedible.

What can I do with it, he sighed, having nowhere to hide it?
I'm afraid that soon a bush policeman might come along
to detain me. I'd make a statement. Say
   I'd like a new bomb, a blue bomb,
a bomb I could explode in dormitories
where my friends are sleeping,
that would not wake them or shake them but
would simply keep them from weeping;
   a bomb I could bounce in the playground
and spray over flowers, a bomb
that would light the Universe for years and send down
showers of joy.

But he'd pay no attention he
would simply take out his notebook and write:
This child is mad.
This child is a bomb.

        *   *   *

Last night in my nightmares
   the bomb became transparent
   and through it my atomic friends wandered, naked
   but for a few carefully placed leaves
   that were continually rotting.

So now looking much older
   I trace about obscure cities
   looking for a place to leave my bomb
   but am always turned away by minor officials
   who say, 'It's a deterrent,' and I answer, 'Sure!'

It will deter
   flowers and birds and the sunlight from calling
   and one morning
   at sunrise when I rise and glow
   I'll look outside to make certain my invention has not bloomed
   but will see nothing through
   the melting windows.

Brian Patten

WHAT WERE THEY LIKE?

1 Did the people of Viet Nam
   use lanterns of stone?
2 Did they hold ceremonies
   to reverence the opening of buds?
3 Were they inclined to quiet laughter?
4 Did they use bone and ivory,
   jade and silver, for ornament?
5 Had they an epic poem?
6 Did they distinguish between speech and singing?

1 Sir, their light hearts turned to stone.
   It is not remembered whether in gardens
   stone lanterns illuminated pleasant ways.
2 Perhaps they gathered once to delight in blossom,
   but after the children were killed
   there were no more buds.
3 Sir, laughter is bitter to the burned mouth.
4 A dream ago, perhaps. Ornament is for joy.
   All bones were charred.
5 It is not remembered. Remember,
   most were peasants; their life
   was in rice and bamboo.
   When peaceful clouds were reflected in the paddies
   and the water buffalo stepped surely along terraces,
   maybe fathers told their sons old tales.
   When bombs smashed those mirrors
   There was time only to scream.
6 There is an echo yet
   of their speech which was like a song.
   It was reported their singing resembled
   the flight of moths in moonlight.
   Who can say? It is silent now.

Denise Levertov

FIVE WAYS TO KILL A MAN

There are many cumbersome ways to kill a man:
you can make him carry a plank of wood
to the top of a hill and nail him to it. To do this
properly you require a crowd of people
wearing sandals, a cock that crows, a cloak
to dissect, a sponge, some vinegar, and one
man to hammer the nails home.

Or you can take a length of steel,
shaped and chased in a traditional way,
and attempt to pierce the metal case he wears.
But for this you need white horses,
English trees, men with bows and arrows,
at least two flags, a prince and a
castle to hold your banquet in.

Dispensing with nobility, you may, if the wind
allows, blow gas at him. But then you need
a mile of mud sliced through with ditches,
not to mention black boots, bomb craters,
more mud, a plague of rats, a dozen songs
and some round hats made of steel.

In an age of aeroplanes, you may fly
miles above your victim and dispose of him by
pressing one small switch. All you then need
require is an ocean to separate you, two
systems of government, a nation's scientists,
several factories, a psychopath and
land that no one needs for several years.

These are, as I began, cumbersome ways
to kill a man. Simpler, direct, and much more neat
is to see that he is living somewhere in the middle
of the twentieth century, and leave him there.

Edwin Brock

TO WHOM IT MAY CONCERN

I was run over by the truth one day.
Ever since the accident I've walked this way
  So stick my legs in plaster
  Tell me lies about Vietnam.

Heard the alarm clock screaming with pain,
Couldn't find myself so I went to sleep again
  So fill my ears with silver
  Stick my legs in plaster
  Tell me lies about Vietnam.

Every time I shut my eyes all I see is flames.
Made a marble phonebook and I carved all the names
  So coat my eyes with butter
  Fill my ears with silver
  Stick my legs in plaster
  Tell me lies about Vietnam.

I smell something burning, hope it's just my brains.
They're only dropping peppermint and daisy chains
  So stuff my nose with garlic
  Coat my eyes with butter
  Fill my ears with silver
  Stick my legs in plaster
  Tell me lies about Vietnam.

Where were you at the time of the crime?
Down by the Cenotaph drinking slime
  So chain my tongue with whisky
  Stuff my nose with garlic
  Coat my eyes with butter
  Fill my ears with silver
  Stick my legs in plaster
  Tell me lies about Vietnam.

You put your bombers in, you put your conscience out,
You take the human being and you twist it all about
  So scrub my skin with women
  Chain my tongue with whisky
  Stuff my nose with garlic
  Coat my eyes with butter
  Fill my ears with silver
  Stick my legs in plaster
  Tell me lies about Vietnam.

Adrian Mitchell

IMPERIAL WAR MUSEUM

brown
horses flopped
sideways in the mud/
khaki uniforms

four years of brown dying
fifty years ago
remembered now
in old
brown
photographs.

Roger Jones

MISSILE COMMANDER

I guess to be spending one's time
spitting cherry-stones into iced
water (counting how many float
and how many sink) might not seem

a task of much high regard for an
ex-Colonel of Infantry
on a missile site. No, sir. But
do you know what better way there

is of keeping a sound fit mind
in a guaranteed, processed-steel,
crap-proof bunker protected from
anything but a direct hit

on Texas? I can tell you there's
a clear blue eye and a fine stiff
upper lip needed for spitting
cherry-stones. Yes, sir. Do you know

that in twelve days, allowing one
spit at dinner one at lunch
per day, the current score (just for
the record) is nearly seven

hundred and thirty-three up for one
hundred and eighty-two down? I
guess in Georgia those red bastards
are pushing around one sixty

five now. According to our checked
latest reports they sure are hard
on our heels. So if you'll excuse
my rudeness I'll just stick with my
conviction we can keep our nose
ahead of those Russkies only
through constant vigilance by our
little bowl of white cherry-stones.

George MacBeth

NORMAN MORRISON

On November 2nd 1965
in the muti-coloured multi-minded
United beautiful States of terrible America
Norman Morrison set himself on fire
outside the Pentagon.
He was thirty-one, he was a Quaker,
and his wife (seen weeping in the newsreels)
and his three children
survive him as best they can.
He did it in Washington where everyone could see
because
people were being set on fire
in the dark corners of Vietnam where nobody could see.
Their names, ages, beliefs and loves
are not recorded.
This is what Norman Morrison did.
He poured petrol over himself.
He burned. He suffered.
He died.
That is what he did
in the white heart of Washington
where everyone could see.
He simply burned away his clothes,
his passport, his pink-tinted skin,
put on a new skin of flame
and became
Vietnamese.

Adrian Mitchell

SOLDIERS

It wasn't hate nor the guns, not the rain
nor the dust, the distress of the villagers, hunger,
thirst, the constant dirt, the cries
of the maimed—a soldier gets used to these;
it wasn't the way a man jerks and slumps
when the bullet hits, the bomb-fragment rips
his useless tunic—such things can be anticipated,
are even expected . . . the weapons were designed
to kill, soldiering is never comfortable,
battles always go wrong for somebody . . .
in the end it was disgust, though first we believed
as children do, in once-upon-a-time,
the good guys and the bad guys, in fairy stories.

Wading through mud in the Delta, we cursed
at the heat, at the flies and the generals, wanted
to prove our mettle; but the enemy wasn't willing,
wouldn't shoot it out, employed and made war
on women, the children, hit us from in front
and behind, from the flanks, laid booby-traps
until we were forced to pretend it was a different
kind of war and found excuses, blamed
the politicians, the terrain and the weather.

And then came the prisoners and the hostages
with their hands behind their heads—sad,
silent, resigned—interrogations, rape,
executions, pillage, burnings and burials.
In between there was booze or the brothel and when
they palled we rolled ourselves sticks, got high,
tried to believe in the ready-made, convenient
lie, set up a mental camouflage, a buffer-zone
to hide and conceal an absence of hope—
what hurt most. We fought and we died
in the way that soldiers do, the way that
is usual, customary, while the heat and the slush,
the stink invaded our clothes and our lives,
heroics seemed merely an opportunist's device—
a pointless display denying desertions
abroad and at home, our disgust, the ague
in the bone. We sweated it out as soldiers
must, until in the end it became plain
and obvious that the enemy and us—both
were portrayed long ago in Rembrandt's picture
of two negroes: one a death's head, the other
wearing that rueful, idiot grin history
has laid incumbent on his tragic race.

Alistair Paterson

NO ORDINARY SUN

Tree let your arms fall:
raise them not sharply in supplication
to the bright enhaloed cloud.
Let your arms lack toughness and
resilience for this is no mere axe
to blunt, nor fire to smother.

Your sap shall not rise again
to the moon's pull.
No more incline a deferential head
to the wind's talk, or stir
to the tickle of coursing rain.

Your former shagginess shall not be
wreathed with the delightful flight
of birds nor shield
nor cool the ardour of unheeding
lovers from the monstrous sun.

Tree let your naked arms fall
nor extend vain entreaties to the radiant ball.
This is no gallant monsoon's flash,
no dashing trade wind's blast.
The fading green of your magic
emanations shall not make pure again
those polluted skies...for this
is no ordinary sun.

O tree
in the shadowless mountains
the white plains and
the drab sea floor
your end is at last written.

Hone Tuwhare

OF LATE

'Stephen Smith, University of Iowa, sophomore, burned what
    he said was his draft card.'
And Norman Morrison, Quaker, of Baltimore Maryland
    burned what he said was himself.
You, Robert McNamara, burned what you said was a concentration
    of the enemy aggressor.
No news medium troubled to put it in quotes.

And Norman Morrison, Quaker, of Baltimore Maryland,
    burned what he said was himself.
He said it with simple materials such as would be found in your
    kitchen.
In your office you were informed.
Reporters got cracking frantically on the mental disturbance
    angle,
So far nothing turns up.

Norman Morrison, Quaker, of Baltimore Maryland, burned
    and while burning, screamed.
No tip-off. No release.
Nothing to quote, to manage to put in quotes.
Pity the unaccustomed hesitance of the newspaper editorialists.
Pity the press photographers, not called.

Norman Morrison, Quaker, of Baltimore Maryland, burned
    and was burned and said
all that there was to say in that language.
Twice what is said in yours.
It is a strange sect, Mr McNamara, under advice to try
the whole of a thought in silence, and to oneself.

George Starbuck

YOUR ATTENTION PLEASE

The Polar DEW has just warned that
A nuclear rocket strike of
At least one thousand megatons
Has been launched by the enemy
Directly at our major cities.
This announcement will take
Two and a quarter minutes to make,
You therefore have a further
Eight and a quarter minutes
To comply with the shelter
Requirements published in the Civil
Defence Code—section Atomic Attack.
A specially shortened Mass
Will be broadcast at the end
Of this announcement—
Protestant and Jewish services
Will begin simultaneously—
Select your wavelengths immediately
According to instructions
In the Defence Code. Do not
Take well-loved pets (including birds)
Into your shelter—they will consume
Fresh air. Leave the old and bed-
ridden, you can do nothing for them.
Remember to press the sealing
Switch when everyone is in
The shelter. Set the radiation
Aerial, turn off your television now.
Turn off your radio immediately
The services end. At the same time
Secure explosion plugs in the ears

Of each member of your family. Take
Down your plasma flasks. Give your children
The pills marked one and two
In the C.D. green container, then put
Them to bed. Do not break
The inside airlock seals until
The radiation All Clear shows
(Watch for the cuckoo in your
perspex panel), or your District
Touring Doctor rings your bell.
If before this, your air becomes
Exhausted or if any of your family
Is critically injured, administer
The capsules marked 'Valley Forge'
(Red pocket in No. 1 Survival Kit)
For painless death. (Catholics
Will have been instructed by their priests
What to do in this eventuality.)
This announcement is ending. Our President
Has already given orders for
Massive retaliation—it will be
Decisive. Some of us may die,
Remember, statistically
It is not likely to be you.
All flags are flying fully-dressed
On Government buildings—the sun is shining.
Death is the least we have to fear.
We are all in the hands of God,
Whatever happens by His Will.
Now go quickly to your shelters . . .

Peter Porter

ASSAULT

Gas
faces turned,
eyes scanned the sky,
hand feverishly rippen open cannisters,
and masks were soon covering faces.
A man choked
as the white cloud,
swirling round him like fog, caught him
unawares.
Then his body flopped over.
Shells floated across
as if suspended by hidden strings,
and then, tired,
they sank earthwards.

A command!
I fixed my bayonet,
scrambled over the open trench
and struggled through
the thick pasty mud.

It was quiet
as we walked
except for the sucking,
groaning, squelching sound
which came from the wet earth
as it tried to
creep into our stockings.
The wind cut me.

Over the wall!
Then a whistle.
  'Good-luck, mates.'
Mind that hole. Through the wire.
Over the top.
And kill.
  'God. This is fun.'

Erno Muller

WHEN THE WAR IS OVER

When the war is over
We will be proud of course the air will be
Good for breathing at last
The water will have been improved the salmon
And the silence of heaven will migrate more perfectly
The dead will think the living are worth it we will know
Who we are
And we will all enlist again.

W.S. Merwin

SOMME AND FLANDERS

Who am I to speak up for the long dead?
Three uncles I never knew say I'm right.
Their tongues are speaking in my head
I'm related to their flesh by fright.

Their world was made of nerves and mud.
Reading about it now shocks me—Haig
Gets transfusions of their blood,
Plum-and-apple feeds them for the plague.

Those Hamsworth books have sepia'd
Their peasants' fields sown with barbed-wire.
In Nineteen-Nineteen, crops of crosses appeared
seeded by bodies ripened in shell-fire.

One image haunts us who have read of death
In Auschwitz in our time—it is just light,
Shivering men breathing rim crouch beneath
The sandbag parapet—left to right

The line goes up and over the top,
Serious in gas masks, bayonets fixed,
Slowly forward—the swearing shells have stopped—
Somewhere ahead of them death's stopwatch ticks.

Peter Porter

Resource Material

Graves, Robert. *Goodbye to all That*. Cape, 1929.
Sassoon, Seigfried. *Memoirs of an Infantry Officer*. Faber, 1930.

Plays.

Littlewood, Joan. *Oh, What a Lovely War*. Methuen, 1965.
Sherriff, R.C. *Journey's End*. Gollancz, 1968.

Novels.

Aldington, Richard. *Death of a Hero*. Chatto & Windus, 1929.
Cummings, E.E. *the enormous room*. MacGibbon and Kee, 1968.
Cloete, Stuart. *Turning Wheels*. Collins, 1967.
Cloete, Stuart. *How Young They Died*. Collins, 1969.
Hemingway, Ernest. *A Farewell to Arms. Cape,* 1929.
Junger, F. *The Storm of Steel*.
Lee, John A. *Civilian into Soldier*. Mayfair, 1963.
Remarque, E.M. *All Quiet on the Western Front*. Putnam, 1929.

THE GREAT WAR 1914–1918

Poetry

Blunden, Edmund (ed.) *War Poets 1914–1918*. British Council and the National Book League, 1958.
Brophy, John and Partridge, Eric. *The Long Trail*. Deutsch, 1965.
Gardner, Brian (ed.). *Up the Line to Death*. Methuen, 1964.
Hussey, Maurice (ed.). *Poetry of the First World War*. Longman, 1967.

History

Blunden, Edmund. *Undertones of War*. Collins, 1928.
Moorehead, Alan. *Gallipoli*. Hamilton, 1956.
Pitt, Barrie. *1918—The Last Act*. Cassell, London, 1956.
Scott-David, David. *World War 1*. Benn, 1965.
Taylor, A.J.P. *English History 1914–45*. The Clarendon Press, 1965.
Taylor, A.J.P. *The First World War*. Hamilton, 1963.
Terraine, John. *The Great War 1914–18*. Hutchinson, 1965.
Tuchman, Barbara, B. *August 1914*. Constable, 1962.
Woolf, Leon. *In Flanders Field*. Longman, 1958.

Autobiography and Biography.

Baxter, Archibald. *We Will Not Cease*. Gollancz, 1939.
Lawrence, T.E. *Seven Pillars of Wisdom*. Cape, 1935.

THE LOST PEACE 1919–1939

Poetry

Bolt, Sydney (ed.). *Poetry of the 1920s*. Longman, 1967.
Rodway, Allan (ed.). *Poetry of the 1930s*. Longman, 1967.
Skelton, Robin (ed.). *Poetry of the Thirties*. Penguin, 1964.

History

Hastings, Paul. *Between the Wars*. Benn, 1968.

Biography

Phillips, C.E. Lucas. *The Spanish Pimpernell*. Heinemann, 1960.

Novels

Hemingway, Ernest. *For Whom the Bell Tolls*. Penguin, 1941.
Hemingway, Ernest. *The Sun Also Rises*. Cape, 1954.
Remarque, E.M. *The Road Back*. Putnam, 1928.

THE SECOND WORLD WAR 1939–1945

Poetry

Blythe, Ronald (ed.). *Components of the Scene*. Penguin, 1966.
Gardner, Brian (ed.). *The Terrible Rain*. Methuen, 1966.

Hamblett, Charles (ed.). *I Burn for England*. Frewin, 1966.
Hamilton, Ian. *The Poetry of War 1939–45*. Ross, 1965.

History

Anatoli, A. (Kuznetson). *Babi Yar*. Cape, 1970.
Churchill, W.S. *The Second World War*. Cassell, 1954.
Eisenhower, Dwight D. *Crusade in Europe*. Doubleday & Co. Inc. 1948.
Liddell-Hart, B.H. *The other side of the Hill*. Cassell, 1948.
Lord, Walter. *The Day of Infamy*. Longman, 1957.
Horne, Alister. *To Lose a Battle*. Macmillan, 1969.
Manvell, Roger and Frankel, Heinrich. *The July Plot*. Bodley, 1964.
Pitt, Barrie. *The Second World War*. Purnell, 1964–66.
Shirer, William, L. *The Rise and Fall of the Third Reich*. Seeker & Warburg, 1960.
Ryan, Cornelius. *The Last Battle*. Collins, 1966.
Ryan, Cornelius. *The Longest Day*. Collins, 1966.
Trevor-Roper, H.R. *The Last Days of Hitler*. Macmillan, 1947.
Whitney, Gen. Courtney. *McArthur: His Rendezvous with History*. Knopf, 1955.

Biography and Autobiography

Brickhill, Paul. *The Dam Busters*. Evans, 1958.
Bullock, Alan. *Hitler—A Study in Tyranny*. Odhams, 1952.
Harker, Jack. *Well Done Leander*. Collins, 1971.
Horrocks, Lieut Gen. Sir Brian. *A Full Life*. Collins, 1960.
Marshall, Bruce. *The White Rabbit*. Evans, 1952.
Memoirs of Field Marshal Montgomery. Collins, 1958.
Mulgan, John. *Report on Experience*. Paul, 1947.
Schnabel, Ernst. *Anne Frank—A Portrait in Courage*. Longman, 1958.
Schnabel, Ernst. *Footsteps of Anne Frank*. Longman, 1957.

Plays

Goodrich, Frances, and Hackett, Albert. *The Diary of Anne Frank*. French, 1954.
Hall, Willis. *The Long and the Short and the Tall*. Heinemann, 1959.
Manvell, Roger. *The July Plot*. Blackie, 1966.
Osborne, Paul. *A Bell for Adano*. (A dramatization of the novel by John Hersey.) Knopf, 1945.
Wood, Charles. *Dingo*. Penguin, 1969.
Wouk, Herman. *The Caine Mutiny Court Martial*. Cape, 1951.

Novels

Cozzens, James Gould. *Guard of Honour*. Longman, 1949.
Davin, Dan. *For the Rest of Our Lives*. Michael Joseph, 1947.
Deighton, Len. *Bomber*. Cape, 1970.

Heller, Joseph. *Catch—22*. Cape, 1962.
Hersey, John. *A Bell for Adano*. Knopf, 1945.
Jones, James. *From Here to Eternity*. Collins, 1952.
Kirst. H.H. *Who's in Charge Here*. Collins, 1971.
MacLean, Alister. *H.M.S. Ulysses*. Collins, 1955.
Mailer, Norman. *The Naked and the Dead*. Wingate, 1949.
Monsarrat, Nicholas. *The Cruel Sea*. Cassell, 1951.
Shaw, Irwin. *The Young Lions*. Cape, 1949.
Shute, Nevil. *A Town Like Alice*. Heinemann, 1954.
Simonov, Konstantin. *Victims and Heroes*. Hutchinson, 1963.
Waugh, Evelyn. *Sword of Honour* (triology). Chapman & Hall, 1955.
Williamson, Henry. *A Solitary War*. Macdonald, 1966.
Wilson, Guthrie. *Brave Company*. Hale, 1951.
Wouk, Herman. *The Caine Mutiny*. Cape, 1951.
Wouk, Herman. *The Winds of War*. Collins, 1971.
Vonnegut Jnr, Kurt. *Slaughterhouse 5*. Cape, 1970.

THE AGE OF ANXIETY 1945—

Poetry

Baxter, James K. *Pig Island Letters*. Oxford, 1966.
Baxter, James K. *The Rock Woman*. Oxford, 1969.
Dorm, Edward and Botheston, Gordon (eds). *Our Word* (guerilla poetry from South America). Cape Golliard, 1968.
Doyle, Charles (ed.). *Recent Poetry in New Zealand*. Collins, 1965.
Hewitt, Stanley (ed.). *This Day and Age*. 1965.
Patten, Brian. *Little Johnny's Confession*. Allen & Unwin, 1967.
Porter, Peter. *A Porter Portfolio*. Scoropin Press, 1969.
Scannell, Vernon. *Epithets of War*. Eyre & Spottswood, 1969.
Sergeant, H. (ed.). *New Voices of the Commonwealth*. Evans, 1968.
Sergeant, H. (ed.). *Commonwealth Poems of Today*. Murray, 1967.
Skull, John (ed.). *Conflict and Compassion*. Hutchinson, 1969.
Perhaps the best anthologies are to be found in the Penguin Modern Poets series.
Especially useful is *The Mersey Sound*. Penguin Poets 10, Penguin 1967. (Poetry by Adrian Henri, Roger McGough, and Brian Patten.)

History

Hersey, John. *Hiroshima*. Hamish Hamilton Ltd, 1947, 1966.
Kennedy, Robert F. *13 Days—The Cuban Missile Crisis*. Macmillan, 1968.
Salisbury, Harrison E. *Behind the Lines Hanoi*. Secker-Warburg, 1967.
Sheehan, Neil. *The Pentagon Papers*. Quadrangle, 1971.

Biography and Autobiography

Yevtushenko, Yevgeny. *A Precocious Autobiography*. Collins, 1963.
Guevara, Ernesto Che. *Bolivian Diary*. Cape, 1968.

Play

Arden, John. *Sergeant Musgrave's Dance*. Methuen, 1960.

Novels

Burdick, E. and Wheeler, H. *Fail-Safe*. Hutchinson, 1960.
Greene, Graham. *Our Man in Havana*. Heinemann, 1958.

Greene, Graham. *The Comedians*. Bodley Head, 1966.
Hess, Dean E. *Battle Hymn*. Peter Davies, 1957.
Knebel, Fletcher, and Bailey, Charles. *Seven Days in May*. Weidenfeld & Nicholson, 1963.
Shute, Nevil. *On the Beach*. Heinemann, 1957.
Solzhenitsyn, Alexander. *For the Good of the Cause*. Pall Mall Press, 1964.
Uris, Leon. *Exodus*. Kimber, 1959.

Every effort has been made to find the publishers of the resource material. The publishers would be grateful for information on the omissions made above.

Index of First Lines

'Action stations.' Tin hats and apprehension   46
A dead youth. How can he turn the heart of a rifle   72
After the next war . . . and the sky   78
All day it has rained, and we on the edge of the moors   52
All the posters on the walls   36
a monstering horror swallows   64
And death shall have no dominion   33
And what have we done with War at last?   9
At dawn the ridge emerges massed and dun   23
At one the Apocalypse had spoken,   64
at the goingdown of the sun   73

Bent double, like old beggars under sacks,   24
Blow out, you bugles, over the rich Dead!   7
brown   85

Camouflaged, they detach lengths of sea and sky   47
'Clearing Black Section   46
Close at my side a girl and boy   31
Continually they cackle thus,   25

Death favoured me from the first, well knowing I could not endure   16
Did the people of Viet Nam   83
Does it matter?—losing your legs? . . .   19
Doll's faces are rosier but these were children   36

Do not despair   44
Do not go gentle into that good night,   32
Down the close, darkening lanes they sang their way   22
Dully she shudders at the solid water   46

Earth opens where the squandered bombs fall wide   51
Enter the fream-house, brothers and sisters, leaving   31

Forget, and forgive them—you say: 21
Four days the earth was rent and torn   11

Gas   90
'Good-morning; good morning!' the General said   19

Have your forgotten yet? . . .   25
Headless, lacking foot and hand,   13
'Here are houses,' he moaned,   12
Here war is harmless like a monument: 31
Here we are all, naked as Greeks,   14
His wet white face and miserable eyes   15
Hooded in angry mist   25
How long, O Lord, how long, before the flood   12
Hullo! here's my platoon, the lot I had last year.   27

I am the man who gives the word,   80
I am the man who looked for peace and found   52
I could not dig: I dared not rob: 9
If any question why we died,   8
If I should die, think only this of me: 8
If I were fierce, and bold, and short of breath,   15
I found him in the guard-room at the Base.   16
I guess to be spending one's time   86
I have a rendezvous with Death   11
I have known old eyes that have seen many more   69
I know a man, he was my chum,   13
'I'm sorry I done it, Major.'   7
In Flanders fields the poppies blow   9
In our heart of hearts believing   7
I saw a picture in the paper the other day   74
I saw a ship come sailing in,   68
I shot him, and it had to be   13
It seemed that out of battle I escaped   23
It wasn't hate nor the guns, not the rain   87
I've lived in the ghetto here more than a year,   55
I was a peasant of the Polish plain;   20
I was run over by the truth one day.   85

I was walking in a government warehouse	77
I was wrong, quite wrong;	13
Just then I saw the bloody Hun.	45
Ladies and gentlemen, this is High Wood,	27
Less said the better	44
Man has the life of butterflies	11
mother the wardrobe is full of infantrymen	74
Move him into the sun—	18
My son was killed while laughing at some	21
Near Martinpuisch that night of hell	14
Never until the mankind making	51
No,	72
No, I'm not afraid of death	13
Nor dread nor hope attend	27
Now, God be thanked Who has matched us with His hour,	8
Now I am still and spent	35
Now in thy splendor go before us,	6
Oh mother my mouth is full of stars	48
Oh what a sobering	75
One day	82
One ever hangs where shelled roads part.	22
On land and sea I strove with anxious care	21
On November 2nd 1965	86
o to be in finland	70
Out of so much talking	72
Out of the smoke of men's wrath,	14
Out there, we've walked quite friendly up to Death;	18
Peach, Plum, or Apricot!	78
Pried from the circle where his family ends,	43
Remember me when I am dead	53
Remember the blackness of that flesh	53
Rocking the cradle of his child	69
Same old trenches, same old view,	18
Say, soldier! Tell us the tricks,	44
Say this city has ten million souls,	37
Sleep now,	76
So Abram rose, and clave the wood, and went,	18
So here am I	55
Soldiers are citizens of death's gray land,	19
Sons of mine, I hear you thrilling	8
So they are satisfied with our Brigade,	15
'Stephen Smith, University of Iowa sophomore, burned what	88
Still falls the Rain—	49
Telling lies to the young is wrong.	80
The boy who volunteered at seventeen	63
The eye behind this gun made peace	45
The flags that were	67
The freighter, gray with rust,	65
The hand that signed the paper felled a city;	33
The House is crammed: tier beyond tier they grin	16
The outcome? Conflicting rumours	77
The past, a glacier, gripped the mountain wall,	32
The Polar DEW has just warned that	89
The roughly estimated ones, who do not sort well with our common phrases,	67
The same old soldiers walking along the same old skyline	76
The winter hardens. Every night I hear	52
Their youth was fevered—passionate, quick to drain	25
There are many cumbersome ways to kill a man:	83
There's a breathless hush in the Close tonight—	6
There set out, slowly, for a Different World,	48
There was a time when I would magnify	70
There will be a rusty gun on the wall, sweetheart,	19
They throw in Drummer Hodge, to rest	6
This bloody steel	20
This excellent machine is neatly planned,	78
This is a damned inhuman sort of war.	51
This is a quiet sector of a quiet front	35
This morning	81
This ploughman dead in battle slept out of doors	16
Those weddings in wartime! The deceiving comfort!	75
3,000,000 is the pricemark on a country	72
Tree let your arms fall:	88
Two neighbours, who were rather dense.	81
Waiting in the bar for the war to end—	48
We ate our breakfast lying on our backs	16
We come from dock and shipyard, we come from car and train,	7
We in our haste can only see the small components of the scene	48
What did you build the trophy of, solider, soldier?	67
What passing-bells for these who die as cattle?	22

When I was kneehigh to a table top,   73
When I was only semen in a gland   70
When nuns were spitted and poets fell   63
When the bloom is off the garden,   45
When the war is over   90
Who am I to speak up for the long dead?   90
Who will remember, passing through this Gate,   35
Why do you lie with legs ungainly huddled,   16

With a dull and hazy light   21
With broken wing they limped across the sky   45
With hatred now all lips and wings   43
With proud thanksgiving, a mother for her children,   24

Yelled, Corporal Punishment at Private Reasons: 74
You said the sun would rise.   71
You would think the fury of aerial bombardment   53

Index of Poets

Aldington, Richard (1892–1962)   11, 13
Appleton, Peter   80
Asquith, Herbert (1881–1947)   25
Auden, W.H. (1907–1973)   31, 37

Bain, Donald (1922–   )   48
Baxter, James K. (1926–1972)   63, 70
Bayliss, John (1919–   )   45
Binyon, Laurence (1869–1943)   6, 24
Bourne, David (1921–1941)   46
Brock, Edwin   83
Brooke, Rupert (1887–1915)   7, 8

Cambell, Roy (1902–1957)   31
Causley, Charles (1917–   )   48
Cervantes, Fernando Gordillo (1940–1967)   72
Cornford, John (1915–1936)   32, 35
Cummings, E.E. (1894–1963)   64, 70
Currey, R.N. (1907–   )   51

Day Lewis, C. (1904–1963)   31
Douglas, Keith (1920–1944)   53

Eberhart, Richard (1904–   )   53
Enright, D.J. (1920–   )   67
Ewer, W.N. (1885–   )   20

Flores, Marco Antonio   72
Frankau, Gilbert (1884–1952)   21

Gibson, Wilfrid (1878–1962)   16, 20
Graves, Robert (1895–   )   9, 14, 74
Guevara, Ernesto Che (1928–1967)   71
Gurney, Ivor (1890–1937)   13

Hamburger, Michael (1924–   )   77
Hampson, Norman (1922–   )   46
Hardy, Thomas (1840–1928)   6, 7
Hawkins, Spike   67
Henri, Adrian (1932–   )   76
Heppenstall, Rayner (1911–   )   52
Herand, Javier   72
Herbert, A.P. (1890–   )   15
Hodgson, W.N. (1893–1916)   8

Ivens, Michael   68

Jarrell, Randall (1914–1965)   48, 65
Johnstone, Philip   27
Jones, Roger   85
Joseph, M.K. (1914–   )   67

Keyes, Sidney (1922–1943)   52
Kipling, Rudyard (1865–1936)   8, 9, 13, 16, 21
Kops, Bernard (1926–   )   78

Lee, Laurie (1914–   )   35
Lehmann, John (1907–   )   78
Levertov, Denise (1923–   )   83
Lewis, Alun (1915–1944)   52

Macbeth, George (1932–   )   86
McGough, Roger (1937–   )   73, 74
McRae, John (1872–1918)   9
Manifold, John (1915–   )   43
Manning, Frederic (1880–1935)   14
Mason, R.A.K. (1905–1971)   69

Merwin, W.S. (1927–   )   90
Milne, A.A. (1882–1956)   18
Mitchell, Adrian (1932–   )   77, 78, 85, 86
Muller, Erno   90

Newbolt, Henry (1862–1939)   6
Newton, Linda   74

Owen, Wilfred (1893–1918)   18, 22, 23, 24

Palmer, Robert (1888–1916)   12
Patten, Brian (1946–   )   76, 81, 82
Patterson, Alistair (1936–   )   87
Porter, Peter (1929–   )   89, 90
Pudney, John (1909–   )   44, 45, 69

Read, Herbert (1893–1968)   21, 36
Rickword, Edgell (1898–   )   12
Rosenberg, Isaac (1890–1918)   12
Ross, Alan (1922–   )   47, 48

Sandburg, Carl (1878–1967)   19
Sassoon, Siegfried (1886–1967)   15, 16, 19, 23, 25, 27, 35
Savage, Patrick (1916–   )   55
Scott, Paul (1920–   )   44
Seegar, Alan (1888–1916)   11
Serraillier, Ian (1912–   )   43
Shanks, Edward (1892–1953)   7
Shapiro, Karl (1913–   )   63, 64
Sitwell, Edith (1887–1964)   49
Sitwell, Osbert   25
Soutar, William   81
Spender, Stephen (1909–   )   36, 53
Starbuck, George   88

Thomas, Dylan (1914–1953)   32, 33, 51
Thomas, Edward (1878–1917)   16
Tuwhare, Hone (1922–   )   88

Weaving, Willoughby   11
Wedge, John (1921–   )   46
Weir, Nigel (1919–1940)   45
Welch, Denton (1915–1948)   51

Yeats, W.B. (1865–1939)   27
Yevtushenko, Yevgeny (1933–   )   75, 80